Roland Berger Strategy Consultants – Academic Network

Titles published in English by the Academic Network

G. Corbae · J. B. Jensen · D. Schneider
Marketing 2.0
VI, 151 pages. 2003. ISBN 3-540-00285-5

S. Dutta · A. De Meyer · A. Jain
G. Richter (Eds.)
The Information Society
in an Enlarged Europe
X, 290 pages. 2006. ISBN 3-540-26221-0

M. Blatz · K.-J. Kraus · S. Haghani (Eds.)
Corporate Restructuring
XII, 180 pages. 2006. ISBN 3-540-33074-7

Burkhard Schwenker
Stefan Bötzel

Making Growth Work

How Companies Can Expand
and Become More Efficient

With 36 Figures

Dr. Burkhard Schwenker
CEO
Roland Berger Strategy Consultants
Am Sandtorkai 41
20457 Hamburg
Germany
burkhard_schwenker@de.rolandberger.com

Dr. Stefan Bötzel
Partner
Roland Berger Strategy Consultants
Am Sandtorkai 41
20457 Hamburg
Germany
stefan_boetzel@de.rolandberger.com

Library of Congress Control Number: 2006937343

ISBN-10 3-540-46486-7 Springer Berlin Heidelberg New York
ISBN-13 978-3-540-46486-0 Springer Berlin Heidelberg New York

Springer is part of Springer Science+Business Media

springer.com

© Springer-Verlag Berlin Heidelberg 2007

Production: LE-TEX Jelonek, Schmidt & Vöckler GbR, Leipzig
Cover-design: Erich Kirchner, Heidelberg

SPIN 11892502   42/3100YL - 5 4 3 2 1 0   Printed on acid-free paper

TABLE OF CONTENTS

Introduction

Corporate growth is the primary goal of management. Growth proves a company's strength but – as we were reminded once again when the e-economy bubble burst – it must be *profitable* growth. Although the importance of profitable corporate expansion is beyond question, it is by no means clear exactly *how* companies can put themselves on a profitable growth path and remain there over the long term. Some companies make enormous efforts to survive the competition and yet still fail to achieve profitable growth. Should we conclude that growth is due to chance circumstances that are beyond the control of companies?

The answer is no. Empirical studies show that some companies manage to follow the growth objective systematically and consistently achieve high growth rates. Evidently, the people in charge at these companies are able to structure the organization and processes in such a way that the existing market demand is converted into corporate growth. For them, management is not a process based on chance but a targeted activity that analyzes opportunities and devises a fitting strategy.

So what is it exactly that these firms do differently? How do they manage to achieve growth? These questions formed the starting point for a number of internal studies investigating the growth phenomenon. Many of us at Roland Berger Strategy Consultants have since investigated this issue, including Partners, members of our elite "Challenge Club", consultants, experts in statistics and our Business Intelligence team. We have analyzed markets and companies, carried out an extensive quantitative investigation of the 1,700 largest companies in the world, evaluated experiences from consulting projects and asked the managers of companies in client interviews how they approach growth. The results have been documented in five brochures, some 60 articles in the daily press and business magazines and in a large number of documents that we have produced exclusively for selected clients. We have also discussed our findings with business people and academics at around 40 events held across Europe. In this book, we summarize our findings to date and develop them in the light of current insights.

The book is limited to selected topics. We believe that successful growth depends first and foremost on companies recognizing a number of basic factors – the essentials, if you like. Here are our basic arguments.

1. The Traditional V Curve No Longer Applies

In the old days it was generally accepted that growth was cyclical. Management focus alternated between periods of aggressive growth and phases of contraction during which the company restructured, saved, or built up its knowledge to help it through the next period of growth. A company's sales or profits figures followed a

V curve – first shrinking, then growing. This way of thinking has survived down to the present day. Indeed, managers often talk about how their company had to tighten its belt during a tough economic period, the implication being that in the following boom they could loosen it again.

Our work with clients shows that this model is outdated. Successful companies combine growth and operational excellence. In this way, they can improve their productivity even during periods of strong growth. In today's fast-moving global economy, companies can no longer afford to take time out to gather their troops and regain their strength. They must continually engage in the battle to keep their processes and structures lean. Only the most agile companies can capture the chances offered by dynamic markets – those plodding along behind will find themselves at a significant disadvantage. Companies must shrink if they want to get fit. This means a major job for companies in terms of motivating the work-force. The teams must be prepared to slim down while working toward growth. They must also exploit reduction potential at the same time as keeping an eye out for growth opportunities.

Growth programs must be based on restructuring, as they must continue even when this goes against the market trend. If companies wait for the right economic conditions to come along, they are wasting precious time. To grow successfully, they should stay on course even during weak economic periods.

2. Corporate Growth Rests on Two Things – The Ability and the Willingness to Grow

There are two prerequisites for growth: the ability to grow and the willingness to do so. Both conditions must be met – a deficit on one side cannot be counterbalanced by a surplus on the other.

The ability to grow relates to all the organizational, strategic and structural aspects of the company. It includes having the right strategy, a suitable legal framework, sufficient liquidity, a competitive portfolio of products or services and the necessary innovation capability. One particularly important aspect is establishing the right value creation structures and capacities. In other words, the question of how the company is organized. As we shall see later, having a decentralized organization substantially strengthens the company's ability to grow. And that's not all: decentralized structures also have a positive impact on the organization's willingness to grow.

The willingness to grow involves what are generally thought of as "soft" factors – things that are, nevertheless, essential to an organization's success. Willingness to grow refers to the attitude of the organization toward growth, in other words the mindset of its workforce and in particular its top managers. This includes their desire to shape the future, their self-confidence and their optimism. It also naturally implies a willingness to take risks, discover new things and champion growth. How the members of top management present themselves is much more important than was thought in the past. Their authenticity, readiness to take on responsibility, discipline, courage and personal integrity function as an example for the rest of the workforce. This example is actively called for today: it is the only way to achieve integration and promote the will to perform in the company, and hence its willingness to grow.

Distinguishing the ability to grow from the willingness to grow allows us to make a precise diagnosis of the situation in the company. It also helps us to choose the right medicine to put it back on its feet – and onto a growth path. In practice, many German companies have the ability to grow but lack the will. They have made the required structural changes. Now they need to adjust their mindset to one of optimism and growth.

3. The Growth Algorithm: Growth Is Self-perpetuating

The end of the V curve and the transition to a parallel strategy set the stage for growth. The growth algorithm can now be set in motion. Excellent operational performance lays the foundations for more free cashflow, which in turn can be used to finance further growth. The resulting economies of scale and scope in turn generate more cashflow, which can again be invested in raising operational performance or further growth. And so the cycle continues.

The underlying principle is clear and simple. However, the real challenge lies in its implementation. In our global study of actual companies, we found that only around one-quarter of companies were able to combine raising efficiency with growth. These companies showed above-average growth and profits growing faster than sales.

That leaves the other three-quarters of companies. These companies didn't manage to set the growth algorithm in motion and keep it going. If they cannot grow as strongly as the market they are at risk of losing market share. At the same time, if they cannot increase efficiency at least as much as their competitors, their margins will come under pressure. By failing to couple growth with increased efficiency, their competitiveness suffers and – in extreme cases – they risk disappearing from the market altogether.

So it's the growth algorithm or nothing: there is no middle ground. Only those companies that follow the dual strategy of growth and increased efficiency can set the growth algorithm in motion and reap the reward of self-perpetuating growth.

4. Flexibility Is the Basis for Growth

The general environment in which business operates has become much more dynamic than in the past. Changes are occurring faster than ever before. Of course, companies can't do much about the external conditions: they simply have to deal with them as best they can. To do this, they must be able to adjust quickly and flexibly. What they need is strategic flexibility – the ability to recognize and react to significant long-term trends before the profitability of their core business is threatened.

Many companies have a hard time accepting that the success formulas they used in the past, or are currently using, do not automatically guarantee a strong competitive position in the future. Moreover, many managers are so caught up in day-to-day operations that they have little energy left for thinking about long-term strategy. Added to this is the fact that successful strategies reach their expiry date much quicker than in the old days. Where previously companies set ten-year strategies, today they are looking at three to five years at best. Strategy guru Gary Hamel identifies four reasons why the pace of "strategy decay" has accelerated:

- *Replication*: Strategies are quickly copied by the competition, losing their distinctiveness and thus their power to generate above-average returns.

- *Supplantation*: Good strategies are always at risk of being supplanted by better ones. In addition, the speed of innovation and thus the level of risk for existing strategies has sped up considerably in recent years.

- *Exhaustion*: Strategies lose significance faster than in the past. This can be due to markets becoming saturated or because customers are more fickle than in the past.

- *Evisceration*: Companies see their lead being eaten up. Customers put their strategy under pressure due to increased transparency or the option of buying products from overseas.

Strategies' shortened shelf-life means that top managers must be constantly on their guard. Careful monitoring of developments on the market forms the best early warning system. Yet, the insights managers gain will not help them if they refuse to accept the necessity of strategic change. Admittedly it's difficult for companies to question existing strategies and business models when they are at the peak of their success. But that's a shame, because in fact the best time for a fundamental review and potential redirection is when the organization is in a growth phase. When profits are falling and cost pressure is increasing, companies usually find their hands tied as far as strategic considerations go. Their main concern is simply to survive the crisis.

The requirement for flexibility not only involves the strategy of a company, it applies equally to the organizational structure. The company must be structured in such a way as to allow a fast, flexible reaction to the changing demands of markets. A rigid organizational structure will be of no use here. So, in addition to monitoring the markets, companies should be constantly reexamining their own structures to ensure that they still provide the best conditions given the market environment and strategy. In our view, the required structural flexibility is best provided by a decentralized organization. Greater flexibility in terms of strategy and organization also requires a high level of qualification and motivation on the part of the workforce – a further challenge that we discuss in Chapter 4.

5. Decentralized, Trust-Based Companies Are the Growth Champions

Trust-based organizations achieve the optimum alignment of ability and willingness to grow. Trust serves as a tool for coordinating the various activities and processes within the company. Staff motivation – the basis for a company's willingness to change – improves as the employees no longer feel that they are tightly controlled within a system of hierarchical relationships. Instead, they see that management really believes in their skills and commitment. Greater structural flexibility also means that companies' growth-related skills improve. And since trust-based organizations can only function properly if they are accompanied by an open, discussion-based culture, the culturally determined aspects of the value creation process, such as innovation capability and customer focus, also improve.

Trust-based organizations have four distinct characteristics: they attach great importance to high-quality leadership; they have decentralized organizations, allowing them to anchor skills in manageable units close to the markets; they have a cultural and organizational framework in which innovations flourish; and they are transparent. This transparency is seen both in their open communication style and in the fact that their corporate governance creates the right conditions for the company to reach its goal of trust, and then constantly checks that this goal is being upheld.

So far, we have only mentioned the internal effects of trust-based organizations. They also have an external effect. They make it possible for stakeholders – business partners, investors, customers, and the general public at home and abroad – to examine how well the company is living up to their specific expectations. Since trust-based organizations are strong, open communicators, investors can expect transparency in the financial reporting, consumer organizations and environmental protection agencies can find out about production conditions, and customers can get information on product quality. This dimension – how the market views the company – is also relevant for growth.

6. Diseconomies of Scale Can Be Overcome

Economies of scale and scope are the result of growth – indeed, in a sense they are its reward. They can be used to stimulate further growth processes. The benefits are relatively easy to harvest. What is more difficult, and requires particular attention from managers, is the avoidance of potential diseconomies. Diseconomies are the disadvantages created by growth processes that prevent the desired benefits appearing in the first place. Examples include disproportionate growth in transaction costs for coordinating a large number of internal and external units, resource-heavy processes for integrating two radically different corporate cultures in a post-merger scenario, and higher administration costs stemming from additional complexity.

Our investigations show that it is vitally important to give such diseconomies due consideration even during the planning stage for growth processes. Companies must ask themselves: can the expected post-merger synergies really be achieved given the conflicting corporate cultures of the two organizations? How should the decision-making process be designed so that it will still function efficiently after the growth phase? And is the technological infrastructure modular, so that the company does not have to meet fixed-step costs before it can grow?

7. Growth Begins with Ambitions

Our analysis of global growth champions shows that companies get nowhere by being cautious. The companies that achieve above-average growth rates consistently set ambitious targets. It appears that high, but not unrealistic, targets actually stimulate growth. On one condition: to be accepted by the workforce, strong targets must be accompanied by moderate sanctions.

In 2004 we carried out a survey of top German and Austrian managers on the subject of growth. We published the results in a study entitled "Managing for Growth". They show that companies achieving above-average growth take a different approach to failure. Surprisingly, strong growth results from ambitious targets in companies where failing to meet these targets is less harshly sanctioned than elsewhere. Our conclusion? Moderate sanctions do not weaken ambition, but rather maintain the pressure that is built up by challenging targets.

These seven arguments form the framework on which we base our discussion of the individual strategies and processes promoting growth. In the first part of the book (Chapters 1 and 2), we present our basic growth model. The second part (Chapters 3 and 4) looks at decentralization and the trust-based organization in more detail. In the third part (Chapters 5 to 7), we analyze the specific conditions that make an organization both willing and able to change. And the final section looks at the broader impact of corporate growth on the economy as a whole.

In the book, we concentrate on the conceptual presentation of the underlying relationships. We show the thinking behind the growth strategies and make practical suggestions on how to implement a successful long-term growth strategy. Our conclusions are supported with findings from our broad-based empirical studies. We have consciously chosen not to present case studies, as these are readily available elsewhere in management literature. Moreover, while case studies often provide useful illustrations, they tend to be rather arbitrary.

Individual companies do not have a monopoly on the growth potential in markets. Any company can get a slice of the action – if their management acts with energy and conviction. Companies should not try to excuse poor performance by blaming adverse economic conditions. The crucial thing is to make the most of the opportunities on the market, both strategically and practically. This is where the true quality of the top management shines through. There are companies in every industry and every area of business that buck the market, making above-average gains in turbulent times. This book discusses the strategies and rules by which these growth champions manage to make growth work.

The End of the V Curve

1. Growth and Continuous Optimization – The Formulas for Sustainable Corporate Growth

Summary:
Growth is the key goal of management. It is not just an indicator of a company's performance, but also the basis for its future success. But growth doesn't just mean getting bigger – it also means getting better. In other words, growth must be profitable, otherwise it destroys rather than increases the company's value long term. And this is not the only challenge. Growth must also be made continuous. The traditional cycle of alternating phases of growth and contraction no longer applies in today's fast-moving economy with its fiercer competitive pressure. In the past companies tightened their belts during lean years when recession hit and loosened them again during years of plenty. But the days when this formula worked are well and truly over: the so-called V curve no longer applies. Today, companies must follow a parallel strategy of growth coupled with restructuring, in the sense of permanently increasing efficiency. These two goals must be pursued at one and the same time. Can this be done in practice? How can management find a successful growth course and stay on it? In this chapter we present our answers to these central questions. We also reveal how the companies that are "growth champions" manage this in practice, as shown by the findings of our study of how the 1,700 largest corporations worldwide manage growth.

Growth Means Getting Bigger and Better

Stagnation means decline. There are plenty of hungry firms out there just waiting to gain ground at the expense of their competitors. The only way a company can prevent this happening is to grow at least at the level of the market – or, better still, grow faster than the market and so gain market share. The advantages of having a large market share – including economies of scale in purchasing, production, and distribution – in turn provide a further stimulus for growth.

Companies must grow, then, in order to establish a permanent basis for their future success. But we are not just talking about growth in a quantitative sense here: high sales figures and a large staff are not assets in themselves. Even titans fall. And there have been spectacular examples of titanic firms going under in all stages of business history – PanAm, WorldCom and Enron to name but three.

Sustained growth rests on a synthesis of quantity and quality. Growth means getting both bigger and better. Only those companies that meet their customers' needs better, invest in innovation and service, penetrate new markets, improve their cost structure and so on are firmly on the path to long-term solid growth. In other words, they can achieve growth that is sustainable and therefore profitable. If this sounds like it should be taken for granted, that is evidently not the case – as shown by a global study of leading firms carried out by Roland Berger Strategy Consultants, whose results we shall come to in a moment. For the moment, let's be clear about one thing: growth is the indicator that a company is pursuing the right strategy with the correct business models and optimum business processes.

The Growth Imperative –
Why Companies Have to Grow

Sales growth has traditionally been the yardstick of business success. Indeed, sales growth is the only lever that allows all of a company's performance indicators – profits, cashflow, total shareholder return, etc. – to be optimized in parallel. It can give firms a clear indication of how they must respond to the market-driven compulsion to grow. But before we look at how growth can be generated, we should briefly identify the key aspects that feed this compulsion to grow:

1) *The demand for increased value:* In simplified terms, the notion of shareholder value is based on a method of discounting future cashflows. Grow these cashflows and you add value. However, since potential returns diminish as a result of constant optimization, over time it becomes less and less possible to generate ever greater cashflows (or, to be precise, free cashflows – net of existing financial obligations) purely from measures to improve efficiency. Higher cashflows therefore require (sales) growth.

2) *Economies of scale:* Learning-curve effects depend on rapid growth. A company can capitalize on the benefits and economies of scale only when it has attained a critical mass. Lower transaction costs and new management possibilities based on improvements in information and communication technology (ICT) are increasingly tilting the balance in favor of large companies and are thus forcing enterprises to either grow or fall behind. We discuss the business implications of this in Chapter 3.

3) *Increasing pressure on margins:* Many markets in industrialized nations are now saturated. Consumers have practically all the consumer goods they need, and industry is well stocked with capital equipment. Increasingly saturated markets erode margins as competition becomes ever more fierce. If sales remain constant, that inevitably leads to shrinking profits. So higher profitability demands higher sales.

4) *Building and maintaining positive prospects:* Only growing companies offer positive prospects to the very best people. International projects, sufficient variation, career development opportunities and excellent compensation packages are the top factors that motivate high performers. These are things that only companies that grow can guarantee long-term. Hence growth makes a company a more attractive employer, as numerous surveys have shown.

5) *The globalization of many lines of business:* Only international businesses are able to operate on a global scale. This is critical because international transactions are growing faster than GDP (see Figure 1). What is more, the real growth markets with high volumes lie beyond the borders of the traditional industrialized countries – namely in China, the ASEAN countries, and specific countries in Central, Eastern and Southern Europe. Companies that currently lack an international orientation must grow if they are to compete successfully on the global stage. Similarly, only companies that produce sufficient quantities of goods in large enough batch sizes can carry out production abroad and so exploit global cost factor advantages.

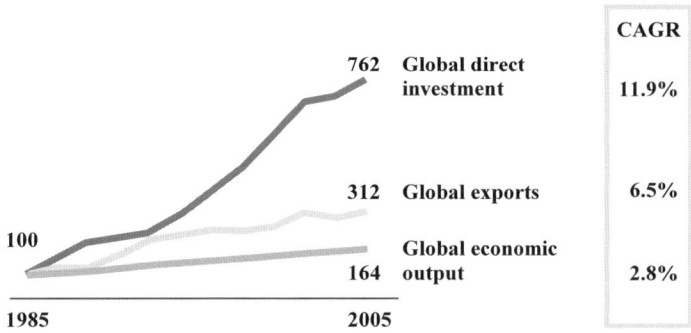

Fig. 1: Global growth rates [1985 = 100] (Source: WTO, OECD, UNCTAD)

Companies can only grow successfully when they have developed a strategy, set appropriate goals to back it up, and agreed it with the organization. This must be part of a fundamental process involving all business units. The strategy should address some key questions: Who are the company's primary customer groups? What business model will be most successful? What trends will affect the sector in future? What products or product innovations could change the market radically? How is the company currently positioned in the value chain? And what position in the value chain does it want to achieve in the future? In this sense, strategy is a long-term (or, at least, reasonably long-term) concept – in spite of the fact that strategic planning's range has shortened as the general environment has become more dynamic.

A company that wants to grow successfully must not wait for the market to tell it what it can, or should, do. It must anticipate developments and trends in the markets – including both the markets where it already operates and the new markets it would like to penetrate. Clearly, then, strategy is not just about copying the patterns that others have followed successfully by others: it is not enough to simply imitate your competitors' best practices. It is generally impossible for a company to repeat the specific approach taken by an established competitor, since one of the following usually apply:

- The competitor provides a service that cannot be readily copied (e.g. Sony, Nokia)
- Its key competence lies in a specific process or product (e.g. Coca-Cola, H&M, Ikea, Aldi)
- It has cornered the market as "first mover" (e.g. eBay, amazon.com, Microsoft, Apple)
- Or it is protected by a strong brand (e.g., Porsche, Harley Davidson, Nike).

As the examples show, companies can achieve the desired success by taking a conscious strategic approach and – most importantly – implementing it consistently. However, this also means that they have to focus in on certain selected areas from among the wide range of possibilities. There is no single recipe for growth, but rather different basic patterns and strategies that must be adapted to the specific (industry or company) context to be fully effective. And companies must keep one thing in mind: a high level of engagement from management is necessary if the growth strategy is to really take off. Growth does not spring up from nothing: it must be actively fostered. And even the most finely honed strategy depends upon the people implementing it for its success or failure. Having the right people in the right places is what brings a strategy to life and makes it successful. The human factor is crucial when it comes to deciding who will ultimately enjoy the advantages of growing most strongly.

The Willingness to Grow

In fact, companies are fully aware of the importance of the human factor. In the spring of 2004 we carried out a survey of top German and Austrian managers. The findings were clear: from the perspective of our respondents, the most important instigators of growth are the people at the top – the board members, CEOs and company promoters. These individuals were ranked far above competences and systems as the key drivers of growth. The reason is obvious: their attitude and behavior lay the necessary cultural groundwork (see Figure 2). Employees can't identify with abstract guidelines – they need human examples. This is what we call a company's "willingness to grow": a supportive culture which connects and involves all the employees and inspires them to walk the difficult path to expansion.

If the employees can get excited about the growth plan, then they will also acknowledge it as a top-down directive and be prepared to commit to it personally.

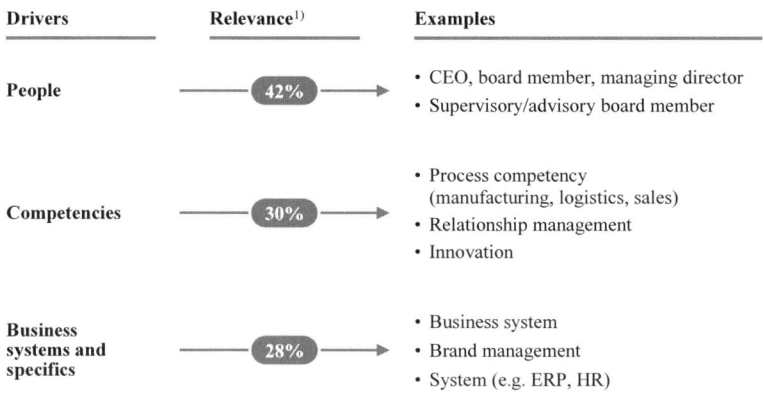

Drivers	Relevance[1]	Examples
People	42%	• CEO, board member, managing director • Supervisory/advisory board member
Competencies	30%	• Process competency (manufacturing, logistics, sales) • Relationship management • Innovation
Business systems and specifics	28%	• Business system • Brand management • System (e.g. ERP, HR)

1) Weighted survey findings

Fig. 2: Key factors in a company's willingness to grow

But that's not all our survey showed. Many companies admitted that practice does not match up to theory. They recognized that their own organizations had significant deficits in the key management components that support growth: staff motivation, top-down targets, personal customer proximity, selection of managers and an innovative corporate culture. Paradoxically, companies appear to lack precisely the high-ranking characteristics promoting growth, while they often display the characteristics that respondents themselves describe as growth inhibitors (see Figure 3).

And there's more. The survey also revealed that companies are often too defensive about growth. Almost half the respondents said that the management of their firms did not give any explicit sign to let everyone in the organization know that they were about to enter a growth phase. This reticence is based on the fear that adverse market conditions will mean they will miss their targets. But our study shows that it is ambitious targets that in fact create the necessary drive – that make the company really put its back into the growth effort. Yes, it's easier to meet low targets, but such targets won't help companies achieve an accelerated growth course. To put it in a nutshell, for companies to grow they must first show the will to grow.

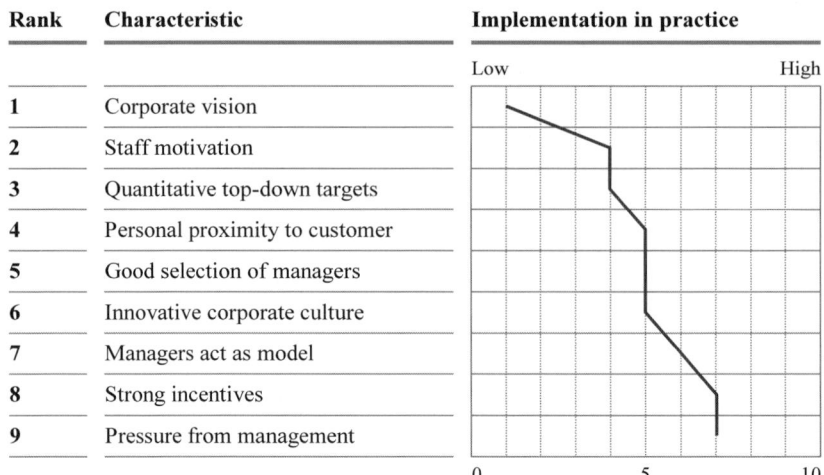

Rank	Characteristic	Implementation in practice		
		Low		High
1	Corporate vision			
2	Staff motivation			
3	Quantitative top-down targets			
4	Personal proximity to customer			
5	Good selection of managers			
6	Innovative corporate culture			
7	Managers act as model			
8	Strong incentives			
9	Pressure from management			
		0	5	10

Fig. 3: Management qualities supporting growth and their implementation in practice

This brings us to a key finding of our study. Companies that want to achieve profitable growth must recognize that their organization, corporate culture and management are the key drivers of growth, and prepare them for growth accordingly. The first step is for companies to examine themselves critically, identifying and dealing with any internal barriers. Once this has been done, growth can begin.

A Further Requirement: Growth Must Be Profitable

One more thing. It's not enough for companies to grow – they have to grow profitably. If they don't, they will fail to generate shareholder value. Hence their growth course must be backed up by a value management system geared toward meeting the following conditions:

- Additional sales must generate profits either by being intrinsically profitable or by helping to make the entire business system more profitable (e.g. through synergies, cross-selling, realization of critical mass, shared services, etc.).

- If the company wishes to increase its value, additional sales must, in line with the value management system, at least earn the cost of capital – the minimum threshold for profitable internal growth. If this condition is not met, extra sales will reduce and ultimately destroy value through unprofitable growth. In the case of external growth through takeovers, the acquisition premium (the difference between the actual value of the target company and its purchase price) must never exceed the forecast synergies – which, of course, must then be realized in practice.

- Growth usually requires investment. The company must therefore have enough free cashflow or be able to free up enough cash through restructuring and optimization in the near future. Alternatively, its debt/equity situation must provide room to acquire new financing. We return to this question in detail in Chapter 6. Essentially, either option means that only profitable companies can chart a growth course.

So growth is important, but profitable growth is even more important. This is an indication of the fact that the market is demanding more and more and expectations on companies are increasing. It is no longer sufficient for companies to meet yesterday's or today's benchmarks – this is no proof that they can hold their own against the competition, nor does it make them attractive for the two resources currently in short supply, investment capital and intellectual input. Today's companies cannot content themselves with being the sales leader in their own sector: only profitable growth can keep them on the growth track in the long run.

The Advantages of Size

Large companies can bring strong advantages to bear. As a result, they enjoy greater growth potential. When it comes to growth, it seems that "big is beautiful". But why should this be so? Here are our answers:

- Companies must achieve a critical mass in order to take full advantage of economies and advantages of scale. Today's sinking transaction costs and rapid progress in ICT mean that diseconomies of scale are disappearing and companies can exploit the economies of scale better. This development – discussed in depth in Chapter 2 – naturally favors large companies. Such companies have an easier time reducing costs, for example by transferring best practices and exploiting learning curves. And lower costs means additional value for the company.

- Large companies find it easier to play an active part in an increasingly integrated global economy. This is because they generally have more funds at their disposal than smaller firms. They can enter and penetrate new markets more quickly, whether off their own back or with the help of their partners. They can also profit more quickly from globalization by exploiting the cost advantages of specific locations. Companies can only go international if they have achieved critical mass. Only then can they position themselves properly in foreign markets and exploit the cost factor advantages offered by certain countries. Moreover, large companies have options in their internationalization strategies that smaller players would find difficult to pull off, such as collaborations and strategic alliances.

- As a rule, large companies have more financial clout than small ones. This makes it easier for them to come up with the money needed for investments either from within the company or by attracting external financing. Although corporate financing by the capital markets is theoretically also available for smaller firms, in practice it is only really viable for large companies.

- A transformation is taking place as we move from an industrial economy, to a service economy, and ultimately to a knowledge economy. In the future, a company's ability to use information – its knowledge – will be crucial for its success. And there can be no doubt that large firms generally have better resources of knowledge than small ones. However, the last ten years in particular have shown that simply having knowledge is not enough. Companies must also be able to transfer this knowledge. In other words, it is how a company applies its knowledge in concrete processes and products that gives it its competitive edge. Knowledge must be applied in order to bring returns in the form of growth.

- In a knowledge economy, a company's greatest capital is the minds of its employees. It thus becomes a matter of supreme importance for companies to attract talented and motivated individuals, and retain them over time. Again, big companies are at an advantage here. High potentials find large firms more attractive as employers than medium-sized companies. Indeed, they even prefer working for large companies to running their own businesses. And this is true not just for continental Europe, but also for the US, where the percentage of people running their own businesses is not higher despite a more widespread entrepreneurial culture.

Naturally enough, all these arguments apply not only to large firms but also to larger medium-sized companies. (The only exception is the last point – here, a change is needed in the mindset of young graduates.) Larger medium-sized companies are also benefiting from economies of scale, going international, making use of the capital market and building on the efficient use of their knowledge (which is often outstanding in their own particular area of specialty). They, too, can leverage economies of scale to achieve more growth and increase efficiency still further. Germany, in particular, has many examples of larger medium-sized firms that are excellently positioned and are enjoying strong growth.

So what about small companies? If they remain isolated, they miss out on all the advantages of scale. If, on the other hand, they can form networks or join virtual organizations, then they too can profit from the scale achieved by this means. As part of a network they can enjoy greater purchasing power, for example through bundling, or share expertise in research and development. Networks also allow small companies to generate economies of scale by having a joint sales platform. However, networks also have their problems in practice. This is perhaps why they are less common than one might expect, given their potential benefits. From a technical point of view, the use of different systems often hampers smooth cooperation. Corporate cultures may also clash, which can be just as much of a prob-lem. What is more, many companies are afraid to work shoulder-to-shoulder with their competitors in case their expertise leaks out and their competitive position is put at risk.

The Growth Algorithm – Starting the Perpetual Motion and Keeping It Going

Growth strategies are a complex matter. As we have already seen, they have to meet a number of targets in parallel: increased sales, value growth, operational excellence and financing growth are all closely interlinked. But there is good news, too. Once a company has found the right "growth algorithm" (this will vary between different companies and industries), growth becomes to a certain extent self-perpetuating. The logic behind this is actually rather simple, especially com-pared to the complexity of defining strategy. Here's how it goes. Operational ex-cellence – shown by greater productivity, falling unit costs, etc. – forms the basis for bigger free cashflows. These can then be invested in growth. As long as growth remains profitable and is properly managed, this in turn generates new, size-related benefits (such as economies of scale and lower factor costs due to globalization). Companies can then use these advantages to generate even bigger free cashflows, and so growth becomes self-perpetuating (see Figure 4).

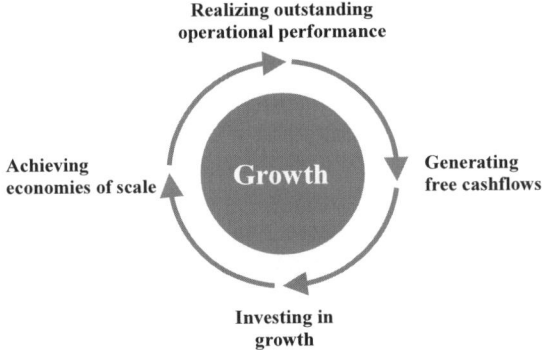

Fig. 4: The growth algorithm

But the pivotal question for business is how to start this perpetual motion going. Well, first companies must bid farewell to the traditional V curve as a manage-ment strategy. This concept was based on the idea that companies develop in cy-cles of alternating efficiency optimization and growth. In simple terms, firms put on weight during years of plenty and slim down during lean years. But nowadays this yoyo pattern is no guarantee of sustainable growth. In today's competitive markets, companies must strive to continuously improve their efficiency, at the same time as growing. Indeed, only a parallel strategy of "growth and restructuring" can bring success in the long term. Incidentally, this sort of restructuring should not be confused with the structural reorganization that can help companies in crisis. In the context of growth, restructuring means modernizing processes and structures with the aim of improving efficiency.

A Global Analysis:
How Do the Biggest Companies Grow?

Over the last two years, we at Roland Berger Strategy Consultants have carried out a number of internal studies to try to identify the best strategies for growth. These studies have dealt with some central questions facing management:

- Is there some formula for growth, or identifiable patterns that make growth processes work?

- What are the critical issues when it comes to developing and executing a growth strategy?

- How must a company be structured and, more importantly, managed to ensure lasting growth?

In an initial quantitative study we looked at the 1,700 top companies in the triad regions: the 900 leading companies in Western Europe, the companies listed in the S&P500 index in the US and the companies listed in the Nikkei-300, effectively the barometer of Japan's stockmarkets. We analyzed the development of all relevant indicators from 1991 through 2005, focusing in particular on sales growth and pre-tax profits, as well as company value (measured in terms of total shareholder return, i.e. share price gains plus dividends). We also examined the operating cashflow, productivity and changes in the number of employees. The period selected by the study spans more than one complete economic cycle, starting with the end of the recession in the early 1990s, continuing through the subsequent upswing and record growth levels across the globe from 1998, and then including the fresh slump in the second half of 2000 and the difficult years from 2001 to 2003 and the subsequent years of upswing again. To minimize the influence on the results of the poor economic years 2001 and 2002, we calculated the mean of the annual growth rates for all values.

And what were the findings of our analysis? The panel's median growth level came to 8.7% p.a. for sales and 17.4% p.a. for earnings before interest and tax (EBIT). Moreover, despite the extreme deterioration in the stockmarket climate that began in early summer 2000, total shareholder return for the world's leading group of companies remained a respectable 14% p.a.

The first thing we see is that, even after adjusting for inflation, the world's largest companies grow faster than GDP on average. Size equals success, if companies want to perform better than the general economy. Of course, this is only an initial, quick analysis. To see the true pattern, we need to dig a little deeper.

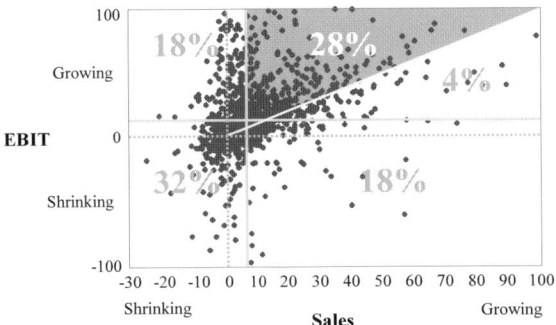

Fig. 5: Changes in pre-tax profits and sales for 1,700 triad companies

To get a clearer picture of how companies performed, we constructed a scatterplot matrix out of the pre-tax profit and sales figures (see Figure 5). We divide the chart into sectors using global averages rather than zero-lines. This gives us a four-field matrix in which the upper right quadrant contains the best companies in the world – those that show above-average growth in both EBIT and sales. Within this group there are also some true stars. We identify them by drawing a diagonal through the upper right quadrant; above the diagonal companies show a higher average rate of growth in their pre-tax profits than in their sales. If growth is supposed to be profitable, then these firms score a perfect ten. Indeed, we might call them "disproportionately profitable". These firms are our *outperformers* (or profitable growers), and they make up 28% of the companies investigated.

Below the diagonal in the upper right quadrant we find the 4% of companies whose growth rates were above the worldwide average, but whose profits grew more slowly than their sales. We call these the *expanders,* and they display considerable potential for the future. If they can improve their operational excellence, they have every chance of joining the ranks of the outperformers. But a glance at the upper right field of the matrix tells an interesting story: many more top companies fall above the diagonal than below it. This means that companies that grow faster than the worldwide average also have a good chance of being disproportionately profitable.

22

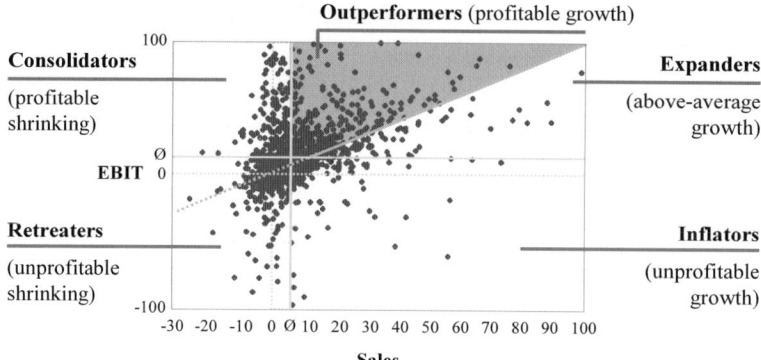

Fig. 6: Five-field matrix showing the development of pre-tax profits and sales

We identify three groups that perform below the overall average (see Figure 6):

- Some 18% of the companies generated above-average sales growth, but were unable to translate this into a corresponding rise in profitability. These are the *inflators* in the lower right quadrant who both destroy value and fail to achieve operational excellence. Sooner or later they will have to prune their growth in order to become profitable. Otherwise they run the risk of slipping back into the ranks of the *retreaters*.

- Just under a third of the companies surveyed saw both sales and profits shrink – with profits falling at an above-average rate in the majority of cases. In other words, these firms did not manage to successfully cut costs to compensate for dwindling sales cause by the difficult market situation. These *retreaters* are caught in a downward spiral and are fighting for survival. Downsizing has not brought about the hoped-for increase in cashflow that could be invested in the growth process. Instead, it has undermined their ability to grow. This demonstrates that permanent cost-cutting can only boost a company's prospects if accompanied by a growth strategy. Without this, companies risk literally saving themselves to death.

- Another 18% of companies managed to grow their profits at an above-average rate despite below-average or even negative sales growth. These *consolidators* (upper left quadrant) are restructuring through a program of downsizing. In the long run, however, this will not create value, as the growth imperative is not satisfied. The firms in this group will need to combine operating cashflows and investment in growth to begin to grow again. If they fail to do this, they will be relegated to retreater level, where they risk disappearing from the market altogether. Indeed, our analyses show that many firms have already gone this way. This is further evidence that the V curve no longer applies: a strategy of pure restructuring, such as that followed by the consolidators, is extremely risky and all too often topples companies into a downwards spiral.

The results of our growth study thus paint a very diverse picture of the growth strategies and capabilities of the largest companies in the global business economy. Only just over a quarter of the companies were outperformers – but these companies outperformed their peer-group in no uncertain terms (see Figure 7):

- The outperformers boosted their sales by an average of 16.7% p.a., compared to just 6.3% for the rest of the companies in the study.

- The outperformers' pre-tax profits rose by an average of 42.7% per annum, compared to a mere 11.5% for the others.

- The value of each company (total shareholder return) in the leading group grew at an average rate of 19.3% p.a., against only 12.7% for the others.

- The outperformers also displayed outstanding results for the other performance indicators. For instance, the average number of new jobs created each year stood at 12.4%, compared with just 3.5% for the other companies (with merger effects factored into both figures). Productivity in the top group rose by an average of 7.4% p.a., against 4.3% for the rest of the panel. Cashflow too – the source of further growth – expanded at an average annual rate of 50.1%, while the other firms could only manage 41.9%.

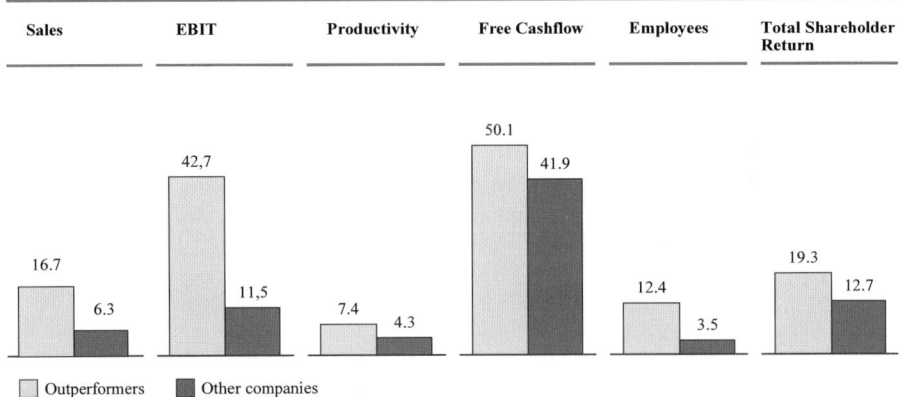

Fig. 7: Average growth rates of 1,700 triad companies between 1991 and 2005 [% p.a., mean value]

Our empirical analysis underscores two important principles. The first is that growth and value creation do not spring out of nothing: the fact that only 28% of all the companies in the study were able to set themselves apart from the rest of the panel reveals the immense importance of good management. The second is that the wide gap between the scores achieved by the leading group and the rest of the field, plus the varying positions achieved in the competitive matrix, indicates potential that remains to be tapped. This leads us to believe that there are future growth opportunities out there just waiting to be grasped.

The European Leadership Model –
Driving Growth on the Old Continent

Comparisons of European companies with companies from other parts of the world – especially the USA and Asia – often emphasize the Europe's need to catch up. Europeans profits are too low, and they pay too little attention to shareholder value. These and similar criticisms are frequently leveled at firms on the Old Continent. Is this true?

If one resists the temptation to "tar them all with the same brush" and instead take a closer, more analytical look at Europe's corporate sector, however, a far more varied picture emerges. A considerable number of European companies are enjoying excellent growth and maintaining a keen competitive edge in the global arena. To find out what distinguishes the successful from the rest was the intention of our competition "Best in European Business" that we conducted for the first time in 2005. Jointly with some of the most renowned universities and business schools, we established a concept and a new methodology to identify and award Europe's most competitive enterprises out of 6,000 companies.

The national competitions in seven countries (France, Germany, Great Britain, Italy, Poland, Portugal, and Spain) identified winners in four categories: growth, value creation, innovation, and strategies for the New Europe. The winners in the growth category posted sales growth in recent years well above that of their respective industries. This assessment also considered whether or not the growth was generated in-house.

Our analysis clearly showed that the winners' impressive performance is actually attributable to these companies peculiarly European approach – what we call the "European leadership model". This model encompasses all aspects of company management, i.e. management objectives, the way in which the company is organized, managed and controlled, and the management culture.

European and non-European companies differ in the leadership models they apply. At first glance, this statement may well raise objections. In the age of globalization, is it not safe to assume that corporate management styles all over the world have long since converged? By no means. Deep-rooted perceptions and practices that have grown up over many decades are extremely resilient. In the context of leadership models, these perceptions and practices notably include different views on stakeholder management, the nature of the goals that guide a company, the precise manner of leading people, and accepted behavior in dealing with collaboration partners. Which are the main characteristics of the European leadership model?

- **Consideration for All Stakeholders and a Commitment to Durable Value Growth**
  Companies operate within a web woven by different groups of stakeholders. Owners, employees, creditors, customers, suppliers, the government, society at large and even the media all pursue their own interests and objectives. These objectives are condensed into the claims and expectations they place on companies. Shareholders, for example, expect the value of the capital they have invested to grow. They are therefore interested in stock price gains and dividend payouts. Employees seek job security.
  When studying the different groups of stakeholders, it is important to understand one principle: Long-term shareholder orientation and stakeholder orientation are not mutually exclusive. Precisely the reverse is true: When a company focuses its actions on sustainably increasing its value, this serves both the interests of the shareholders and those of all the other stakeholders. This combination – reconciling the need to increase company value in the long term with consideration for the interests of all stakeholders – is a typically European approach.

- **Empathizing with Collaboration Partners and Customers**
  European companies have one crucial factor in common in the way they approach the outside world: They are all accustomed to working with companies from different cultural backgrounds and with different languages. Back in the days when national borders were perhaps more important than they are today, this skill was vital if companies were to realize economies of scale and put cross-border clusters to profitable use. The ability to empathize with all kinds of different collaboration partners naturally benefits European companies not only "at home" in Europe, but also throughout the globalized economy.

- **Corporate Social Responsibility as an Integral Part of the Corporate Culture**
  Today's companies can no longer afford to ignore the world around them and concentrate solely on maximizing their profits. Public opinion and the influence of the media have grown too powerful: The impact of such corporate action would no longer go unnoticed. Defective products, pollution of the environment, the manipulation of balance sheets and other forms of managerial malpractice are brought to light very quickly and can do enormous damage to a firm's reputation. The only thing that helps is transparency and collaboration in respect of all company's shareholders. We have already noted how important such collaboration is – and the enviable position enjoyed by European companies on this score.

We are convinced that the European model holds out the promise of greater success. We believe that a focus on sustainability and the willingness to factor all stakeholders' interests into corporate strategy will pay dividends in the long run. Therefore, Europe's companies need not fear comparison with firms from other regions of the world. On the contrary, certain aspects the European leadership model give the region's indigenous companies a clear advantage in international competition. Even more importantly, Europe already has enterprises that possess the skills they need to enjoy lasting competitive success. Many of these skills are either specifically European capabilities, or they are hard to copy. Either way, they constitute a competitive advantage. As market conditions continue to change, European companies must nevertheless consistently develop and improve in order to consolidate and build on their lead. In other words: They have to pursue the strategy of growth and continuous optimization.

Different Paths to Growth

In practice, we can observe companies taking a wide variety of paths toward achieving their growth targets. As part of our comprehensive investigation of the growth question, we have attempted to bring this variety into some sort of order. Traditionally, growth is achieved internally or externally. More recently, we have also observed the rise of growth via partnerships between companies. Here are the details:

- *Internal growth:* Typically, internal or organic growth is realized on the basis of the company's own strength and using its own resources. By definition, internal growth takes place without acquisitions. But relatively small acquisitions, involving sales organizations or production plants, for example, can generally still be considered part of an organic growth strategy. Internal growth strategies of this kind are usually less risky. However, organic growth usually requires the company to take a longer-term perspective, as the processes need more time and do not result in sudden leaps forward in growth.

- *External growth:* This includes all strategies in which growth is achieved by buying in external resources. Mergers and acquisitions allow a company to make substantial advances in growth within a short space of time. The factors that motivate such strategies are obvious: swift penetration of new market segments, consolidation of saturated markets, internationalization of business activities and vertical or horizontal integration along the value chain to improve the company's cost position. Growth via acquisition is also a natural choice where a company wishes to acquire an established brand or buy in expertise.
  External growth tends to happen in leaps and bounds, and some mergers have doubled sales at a stroke. But external growth strategies also harbor

enormous risks – the figures on failed mergers or shrinking value following fusions speak for themselves. The special feature below examines some of the risks and success factors associated with mergers.

- *Growth via partnerships:* In the traditional approaches described above, companies try to incorporate growth within the limits of the existing company. They either build growth from within, or they buy growth in. However, many companies have been taking a third approach of late: they set up project-specific (or target-oriented) alliances with the aim of achieving "virtual growth". This strategy boils down to farming out part of the value chain – which, of course, fits in well with a policy of concentrating on core competencies. Accordingly, they expand their use of external service providers or join forces with a strong partner on the sales side who can distribute their output effectively on the market. This is a good growth strategy particularly for companies wishing to expand internationally, or who want to offer packages of products and services.
The advantage of such an approach is that the entrepreneurial risk is split between the two partners and growth does not have to be supported by either partner on its own. The arrangement between the two companies can also be flexible, depending on how the contract is drawn up between them.
"Virtual growth" via partnerships is made possible by two key factors: global economic integration and technological integration. The removal of barriers to trade and investment, coupled with growing legal stability, has made international relationships between companies much easier, and in some cases possible for the first time. Moreover, information technology infrastructures can now better manage and control the division of labor (even on an interregional basis). Since more fundamental innovations are on their way in this field, we should expect to see further structural changes reshaping the business landscape. In this context, the concrete opportunities for growth hinge on the question of whether collaboration really can provide an adequate answer to existing size-related limitations.

Special Feature: Cold Calculation, Not Euphoria –
The Success Factors Behind Growing and Enhancing Value
Through Mergers

The 1990s saw a continuous rise in the number of mergers between companies. This wave peaked in the year 2000, when there were over 13,000 mergers (with publicly announced purchase prices) representing a total volume of more than EUR 4,000 billion. But the euphoria didn't last. Soon afterwards, reality kicked in, as companies realized that they had overlooked a number of risks:

- The strategies behind the mergers hadn't been thought through properly

- There were culture clashes between the newly merged companies

- The hoped-for synergies didn't materialize, or were a long time coming – i.e. the acquisition premium turned out to have been too high.

This last point in particular lay behind the ultimate failure of many mergers. Companies had overestimated the potential synergies and gotten caught up in the euphoria, rather than proceeding with the proper care and caution. Indeed, the success of mergers hinges on a number of unknowns, all of which influence the synergy potential. How stakeholders (customers, staff, shareholders, etc.) will react to the merger is just as much of an unknown as the reaction of competitors. The company may end up being forced to pass on the synergy potential to its customers. And focusing on the merger can lead companies to neglect the running of their day-to-day business. Also, it is all too easy for companies to make mistakes when calculating the potential synergies. This is, after all, a somewhat subjective matter. And companies must not forget that they are working against time when it comes to realizing the synergies: as a rule they only have two to three years to realize the potential of the synergies. This comparatively short time-span makes it particularly important that companies quantify the synergies accurately, and then put all their energy into quickly realizing them in the initial period after the merger. At the same time, they must not neglect their day-to-day operations or lose sight of the longer-term cultural implications of the merger.

After the year 2000, the level of mergers initially fell drastically, both in terms of the number of deals and their volume. Thus, in 2003, the volume had slumped to one-third of its record year 2000 level.

Things have picked up again since 2004. There are clear signs that takeovers are back in fashion, and sometimes on a grand scale. Sanofi-Synthélabo started the ball rolling with its acquisition of Aventis. This was followed in 2004/2005 by mergers in the software industry (Oracle acquiring Peoplesoft), telecommunications sector (Sprint acquiring Nextel) and electronics sector (Honeywell acquiring Novar).

Driving these new fusions is the old hope of realizing synergy effects and penetrating new markets. Growing profits mean that more money is available for acquisitions. At the same time, the level of trust in company supervision, both internal and external, has increased, creating a better climate for mergers. The supervision of stock exchanges has become stricter and corporate governance guidelines have been tightened up. As a result, companies are less worried today about falling victim to "creative accounting" or paying fancy prices far in excess of the real value of the target company.

Today's merger decisions have a more solid basis than during the hype of 2000. Indeed, this is a major factor in the current upswing in the number of takeovers. Acquisition prices have normalized as companies are taking a less euphoric, more realistic view of the benefits of a potential merger. This is reflected in lower prices on the stock exchange. Today's managers are also better prepared to shape a merger successfully. They have learned from past mistakes – mistakes that led to the failure of many mergers – by analyzing carefully what exactly went wrong. It has been a hard lesson to learn, but it has meant that they now know what it takes to make a merger successful:

- The acquisition must fit in with the company's overall strategy. Growth in size terms alone, whose only effect is to give the firm's leaders greater clout, is leading the company up a blind alley.

- Looking at the absolute value of synergies is not enough: the time-span within which they can be realized must also be taken into consideration. Acquisitions that only promise to deliver synergy effects in the medium term should be looked at especially critically.

- Supposedly "soft" factors – management style, communication, HR – can be just as important as hard factors for the success of an acquisition. The acquiring company must first be fully aware of its own culture, and then take a close look at the culture of the target company. In fact, the two cultures do not have to be identical: it can even be more advantageous if the cultures are complementary. Moreover, both soft and hard factors should be examined by a third party, not by the company itself.

- Before the merger takes place, the company should think about the future relationship between the two companies. This applies to hard as well as soft factors. If the acquired company is to preserve a high level of autonomy, cultural differences will be less important than in a complete fusion for example. A gradual integration of the two companies is also possible – indeed, this is often more successful than immediate integration and it makes it easier to remove any parts that do not fit in with the newly merged company.

- Shareholders' interests are important, but they should not be the only consideration in mergers. Other key stakeholders – clients, staff, suppliers – must be given equal attention. For them, the merger will automatically mean a loss of security at first. This makes proper communication with stakeholders of paramount importance.

- Alternatives should be investigated. These include not just growing on the company's own strength: collaborations, or acquiring a minority interest in another company can bring similar results to a takeover, and with much less risk.

Basic Strategies for Growth Processes

The three basic growth patterns – internal growth, external growth, and "virtual growth" via partnerships – provide the framework for companies to define their own individual growth strategies. Based on our experience from consulting projects and our global surveys, we identify six basic strategies for growth processes employed by companies around the world. These are discussed in turn below.

Growth Through Improved Market and Customer Penetration

This growth strategy works within the existing business system or delivery program. The usual measures to this end include branding or changes to marketing policy (line extensions, relaunches, brand profiling), the introduction and intelligent use of CRM systems, improvements in the sales organization and so on.

However, this kind of activity generally serves only to safeguard the market position a company has already achieved. At best, it might lead to a slight increase in market share. Accordingly this strategy normally only delivers growth in small increments. It is quite a different situation if a company manages to change the rules of the game in its own favor – for example by setting new standards, supplying add-on offers or developing new business models.

An example of a company that has managed to do this is the Greek mobile phone operator Cosmote. As "third mover" it was able to achieve market leadership within a short space of time by developing services for the mass market – until Cosmote came along, mobile telephones had been considered a business market product in Greece. In a similar way, the market for air travel has been turned upside down by low-cost carriers such as Ryanair, easyJet and hlx.

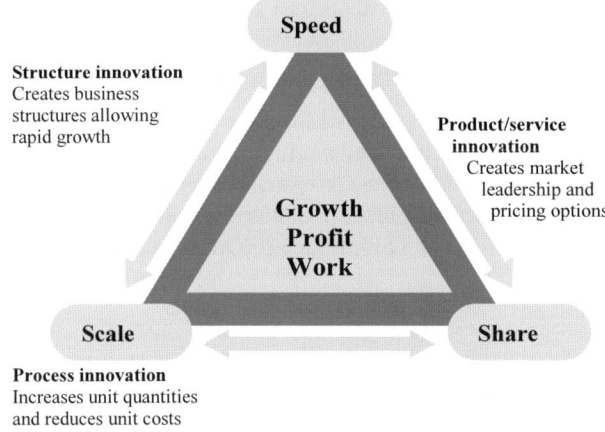

Fig. 8: The three Ss for innovations

Growth Through Innovation

In this strategy, growth is generated by the development and launch of new products. As long as innovation is based on in-house development by the company, the crucial skill here is to master the so-called "3S" process (see Figure 8). Step one is to ensure speed in bringing the innovation to market. The quicker this is done, the more first-mover advantages the company can enjoy. First-mover advantages allow a company to gain a significant market share, which can in turn be invested to realize economies of scale. Of late, a new growth strategy has emerged here: instead of developing innovations in-house, companies are increasingly buying in market-ready innovations, particularly in the fields of software and biotechnology.

Apple is an example of outstanding innovation and excellent customer focus. In its computers as well as its other products (such as the iPod portable music player), Apple successfully combines innovative technology with innovative design. Nestlé is another good example of a company successfully realizing new growth potential through innovation, for example in the area of nutritional products.

Growth Through Globalization

This strategy involves a company overcoming the limitations to growth inherent in the markets in which it already operates and taking its business international. This can be motivated by various factors, depending on the individual situation of the company. Some companies, for example, globalize because a customer that they act as supplier to sets up a new production plant abroad, and they need to follow. Others hope to win new customers in volume and growth markets themselves. Still others hope to reduce unit costs by exploiting cost differences in goods and factor markets in different locations, or by improving their logistics position. And some companies want to access international expertise so that they can get a lead in innovations.

Examples of firms successfully growing through globalization are Carrefour, the leading European food retailer, and Citigroup, the only globally successful retail bank. Similarly Vodafone, with its long-term worldwide expansion strategy, has become the only mobile network operator that is truly globally active.

Growth Realized by Focusing the Company's Portfolio and Concentrating on Core Competencies

This strategy takes two forms. The first is where a company restricts itself to certain segments in which it has the potential to become market leader, and jettisons its other divisions. Alternatively (or in addition) the company concentrates on the parts of the value chain where it is particularly strong – i.e. it carries out vertical disintegration. In both cases, companies can thus leverage their specialization or experience to arrive at a superior unit cost position and generate higher margins. This also has the welcome effect of rationalizing their portfolio, and they can use the money freed up to finance further growth. How this works exactly is explained in Chapter 6, where we investigate how companies can finance growth.

RWE and E.ON are examples of this strategy in action. They have consistently focused their portfolio on multi-utility business with an international focus, while non-core areas such as telecommunications have been sold off. Another example is Flextronics, who increased their sales several hundred times over during a period of seven years by manufacturing chips on behalf of hardware producers under outsourcing arrangements. And Porsche has the least vertical integration of all automotive manufacturers and so achieves a maximum of profit.

Growth Through Active Market Consolidation

This strategy aims to consolidate the market by means of mergers and acquisitions, and thereby exploit cost advantages through growth. The way this works is clear. Market consolidation forms the basis for removing surplus capacity. Improved capacity utilization then optimizes the cost of the products and services on offer. Saturation in many major sectors is not the only trigger here: there are also external factors, such as the politically motivated opening up and deregulation of markets and rapid progress in future technologies. Outperformers ensure they are at the forefront of such developments and, on the basis of this position, they achieve superior growth. Take Total Fina Elf, for example. It has employed a successful strategy of mergers and acquisitions and managed to turn itself into the only firm in continental Europe that belongs to the group of leading oil producers, which is otherwise dominated by Anglo-Saxon players. Likewise Volkswagen has bought up European competitors such as Seat and Skoda and thus contributed to the consolidation of the market.

Growth Through Network Development

In this strategy, a company aims to generate relative advantages that will enable it to serve existing markets better (e.g. product improvements, innovation) or win new customers. This strategy offers a wide range of options – here are just a few examples:

- Collaboration in research and development (often in the automotive and pharmaceutical industries)
- The definition of common standards that raise the barriers to market entry (often in technology-based segments such as IT, telecommunications, consumer electronics, multimedia, etc.)
- The integration of external service providers to round out the product offer, or the creation of a "one-stop shop" at the front-end with a number of partners working in the background
- The merger of customer bases and creation of joint offers (bonus and purchase programs).

The fast-growing, knowledge-intensive markets of the past decade (information technology, biotechnology and biopharmaceutics, high-tech applications, etc.) made it necessary to combine highly specialized knowledge not only on a technical level, but also in relation to end customers. The formation of networks along the value chain thus became the principal driver of growth. SAP, for example, has created a unique network of service-provider partners around its software applications, thereby safeguarding its market leadership.

Networks have also sprung up in the more traditional sectors. Star Alliance has shown how a partnership can boost the marketing strength and profitability of its members if their efforts are truly customer-centered. Star Alliance has been immensely successful in setting up a joint network of air routes, introducing common service standards and boosting customer loyalty. The synergies achieved have also meant that the individual airlines could optimize their costs. And branding has also profited from the creation of the network: today, the Star Alliance brand is established worldwide.

The Dual Effect of the Growth Strategies

As we have already seen, successful growth is only possible nowadays if a company continuously improves both on the cost and the process side. These two areas must be optimized in parallel. The previous approach of first restructuring, then growing no longer functions – faster-moving markets, higher investor expectations and increased transparency make this impossible. All the more important, then, that the chosen (combined) strategy aims at the same time at both expansion and excellence. These two goals must be pursued in tandem if a company wishes to achieve business success in the medium and long term. Pursuing one goal in isolation will bring, at best, short-term success.

Growth		Costs
Improved sales	Market/customer penetration	Economies of scale, cashflow
Differentiation, technical edge	Innovation	Cost cutting (process innovation/productivity)
New markets	Globalization	Factor cost advantages
Better performance due to partnerships, concentration on core competencies	Outsourcing	Reduction of fixed costs, replacing fixed costs with variable costs
Increased market share	Market consolidation	Economies of scale, cashflow, productivity increases
Access to new markets and/or customers	Network development	Balancing out diseconomies

Fig. 9: The impact of the six basic strategies on growth and costs

What this means is that companies must constantly accompany their growth efforts with measures aimed at improving efficiency. This is where the six basic strategies come into their own (see Figure 9). Our survey findings back this up:

the outperformers have clearly mastered the "trick" of following a dual strategy, and it is this that distinguishes them from the competition.

Some examples will help here. This is how the basic strategies can be effective in two directions at the same time – promoting growth and improving efficiency:

- Improved *market penetration* focuses on growth. However, it also has elements that impact on costs. For example, it can be used as a lever to make the sales organization more efficient or to optimize costs as part of new pricing measures.

- *Innovation* has elements that impact on growth. It can be used to differentiate a company from the competition and thereby give it a competitive lead. The same applies for new business models – here, an optimized sales approach can lead to expansion. Innovation also has an effect on costs: processes innovations and technological progress improve operational performance.

- *Globalization* enables a company to exploit global factor cost advantages. Practices such as global sourcing, global production configurations, and/or the cost-induced closure of domestic sites make the competitive position more competitive on the cost side. This promotes operational excellence, which plays a central role in generating cashflow. At the same time, globalization lays the groundwork for expansion, opening up new markets and hence enormous potential for growth.

- Active *market consolidation through mergers and acquisitions* improves a company's cost and margin position. On the basis of this position, it enables the company to grow and invest the additional cashflow in further improving its own future growth capability.

- As we have seen, *networks* are a highly effective strategy for minimizing growth deficits as regards access to customers or know-how. If used properly, they can also compensate for a company's smaller scale and so also have an effect on the cost side.

- Measures aimed primarily at reducing costs can also have strategic relevance for growth. *Focusing portfolios* is a good example: it frees up cashflow by eliminating activities that are not part of the firm's core business, thereby improving productivity. The funds thus realized can then be invested in areas of growth or in expanding core business activities.

Of course, whether these measures are actually effective in both directions – sinking costs and promoting expansion – depends crucially on the timing. If restructuring is desperately needed because the company has hit a financial crisis, the cash that is freed up by cost reductions cannot be invested in growth. Instead, it will have to be used to service legacy obligations (loans, etc.), so it does not create any prospect of growth. True, such measures ensure the short-term survival and profitability of the firm. But having done that, the company will have to accumulate the newly earned profits to generate the cashflows that can finance investment in the future. In the best-case scenario, precious time is lost. And in the worst-case scenario, the company is caught in a downsizing spiral from which it will not be able to escape.

The only strategy that promises long-term success is for ongoing (cost) optimization to generate enough free cashflow to tap areas of growth. Raising efficiency and expansion must occur in parallel. And that makes finding the right combination of *cost-reducing* and *growth-promoting* measures a matter of paramount importance.

2. Overcoming the Limits to Growth – Exploiting Economies of Scale and Scope

Summary:
As every manager knows, economies of scale and scope are a company's growth bonus. However, growth can also have a flipside. It can bring diseconomies in its wake that put the brakes on the growth process. Avoiding diseconomies of scale and scope, or at least limiting their destructive potential, must come right at the top of management's agenda. This includes recognizing the danger of diseconomies already in the planning stage of growth processes, and taking the necessary counteraction. These days this is easier than in the past: transaction costs, which play a key role in creating diseconomies of scale, show a clear tendency to fall. And this is giving companies great new opportunities to throw off the shackles of diseconomies and exploit the advantages to the full.

Falling Transaction Costs Are Creating New Economies of Scale

Economies of scale and scope are the result of growth – if this growth is properly managed. In a sense they are its reward: they are efficiency advantages that allow companies that have achieved sufficient critical mass (exactly how big depends on the type of business) to improve their operational performance and efficiency even further.

At the same time, achieving economies of scale and scope releases the energy for additional corporate growth. They create an improved basis for generating additional free cashflows, which can in turn be invested in further growth and better operational performance. This makes them drivers of the growth algorithm and the basis of the parallel strategy based on growth and cost reduction.

However, this mechanism cannot be milked *ad infinitum*. When a company grows beyond a certain size, there is an increased risk that the economies of scale will be outweighed by the so-called diseconomies of scale. One of the chief causes of diseconomies of scale are transaction costs – the costs involved in coordinating business activities. Transaction costs include, by definition, the cost of initiating, agreeing, monitoring and modifying business transactions. They arise both within a company and in business activities between partners in the marketplace. Together with production costs, they make up the total cost of a product.

38

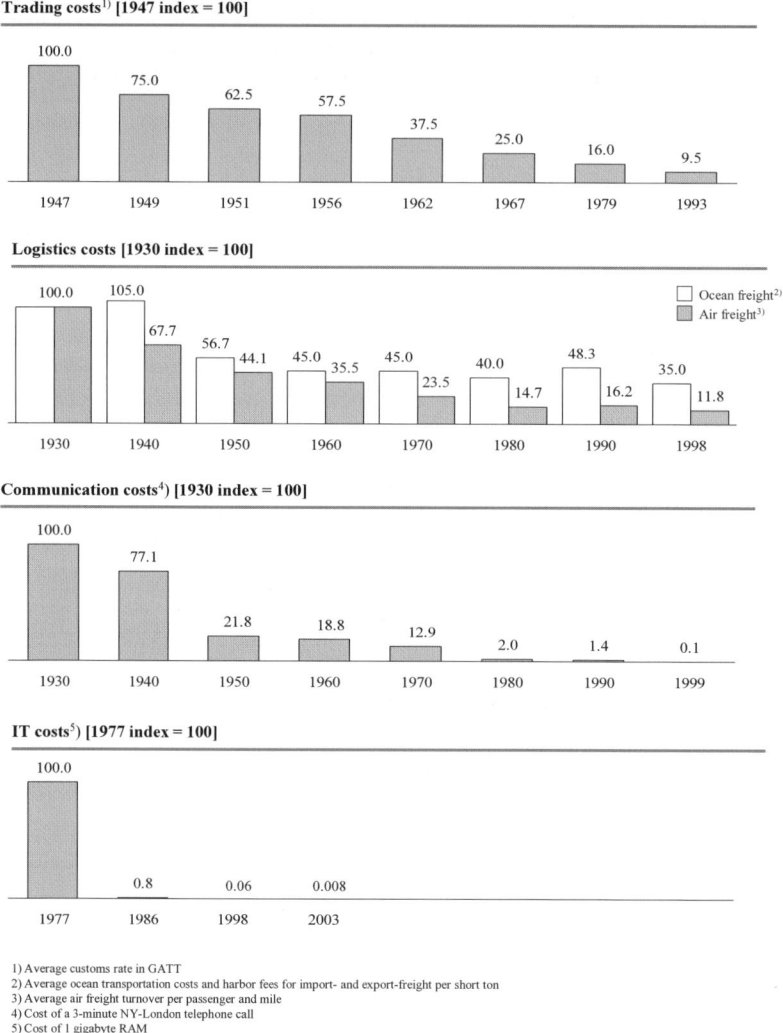

1) Average customs rate in GATT
2) Average ocean transportation costs and harbor fees for import- and export-freight per short ton
3) Average air freight turnover per passenger and mile
4) Cost of a 3-minute NY-London telephone call
5) Cost of 1 gigabyte RAM

Fig. 10: Historical development of transaction costs (Source: HWWA, TimesTen)

Transaction costs play a central role in determining the limits of profitable growth for a company. As the company grows, so does the cost of coordinating its activities. This continues until the point where the coordination costs tip the balance, outweighing the economies of scale. Here it is worth noting that we are currently in a phase in which transaction costs are falling successively, as confirmed by numerous indicators (see Figure 10):

• Information and communication costs have plummeted while hardware and software capabilities have soared. The massive expansion in infrastructure and the competition that has evolved in the wake of liberalized telecommunications combine to squeeze prices. The standardization of services as well as hardware and software reduces the number of interface problems, enables networking economies and thereby cuts costs

- Logistics costs – for air and ocean freight, for example – have declined radically in recent years.

- Multinational trade agreements – such as GATT and WTO – and bigger free economic zones like the EU serve to cut customs duties and reduce non-tariff barriers to trade.

This development opens the way for companies today to expand on a previously unthought-of scale. At the same time, they can now exploit the economies of scale and scope much better than before. The connection between transaction costs and optimum company size is shown in Figure 11. Both charts show that positive economies of scale are generally realized in production costs. In other words, the average production costs sink as production volume rises. This is particularly due to the successive reductions in fixed costs. In the past, on the other hand, transaction costs grew disproportionately as output went up, as shown on the left-hand chart. The optimum company size is reached when the unit costs – that is, the sum of average production and transaction costs – hit their lowest level. But if transaction costs fall, as has happened in recent years, the minimum unit costs can be achieved for larger output. And when this happens, the ideal company size increases and the line shifts to the right, as shown on the right-hand chart.

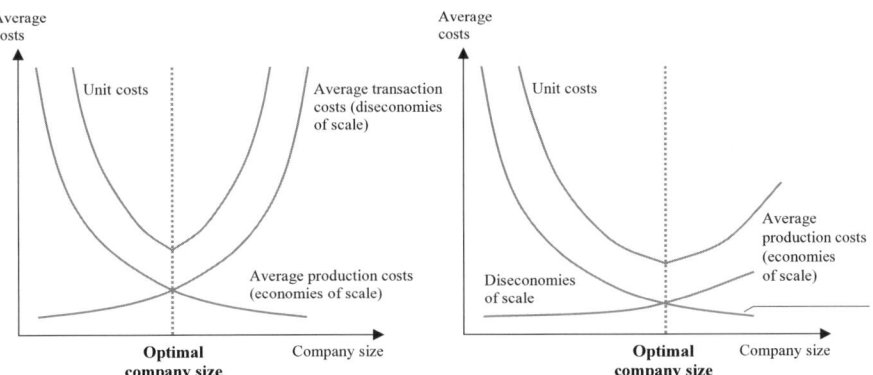

Fig. 11: Companies can grow larger by reducing diseconomies of scale

So with sinking transaction costs, today's companies can grow larger than ever before. And as companies grow, so does the importance of economies of scale. In business terms, economies of scale are what you get when unit costs decline as output rises. Internal economies of scale can be achieved – as every manager learns in their first semester at college – when the productivity of machinery is optimized, when price discounts are obtained on bulk purchase orders or when a company is granted better terms on a loan due to the size of its organization, for example. External economies of scale come into play when companies profit from the geographical concentration of their industry or from local population density. In that case they have access to a wide range of suppliers, partners and potential new employees and can take advantage of better government infrastructure, such as roads, universities and schools. Economies of scope likewise occur when producing two different products together is cheaper than producing them separately. These kinds of synergy effects frequently result from the joint use of centralized functions or the use of the same machinery platform in the manufacturing process.

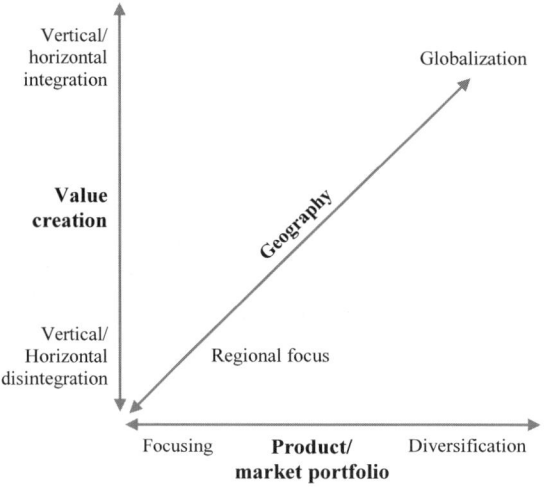

Fig. 12: Economies of scale and scope can be realized in three dimensions

These interrelationships are hardly news – indeed, they are described in every handbook on management. Yet when we look at companies in practice we find that problems evidently begin when it comes to implementation. Today's companies all have full access to the latest management theories. But despite this we find significant differences in the cost structures of comparable companies. Differences occur in the level of cooperation within the organization, the quality and speed of decision-making processes, and the level of honesty – both with regard to benchmarks and internally. These, it seems, are the decisive points where companies succeed or fail in turning theory into practice.

Before we go any further, it is worth defining exactly what areas companies should be focusing their analyses on. Economies of scale and scope do not appear as if by magic. In order to realize their full potential, three dimensions need to be carefully considered (see Figure 12):

- Value chain coverage: Integration versus disintegration

- Regional alignment: Concentration versus expansion
- Product/market portfolio: Focusing versus diversification

Determining the Degree of Vertical and Horizontal Integration

In principle, economies of scale and scope can be realized at any point in the value chain. This is particularly true today, when it is simpler than ever before for companies to "deconstruct" their value chains, breaking them down completely and then reconstructing them in an optimized form. Companies can split different parts of the chain between internal units and external partners. Increasingly, they also have the option of choosing global partners by means of offshoring. In this way companies can determine the particular value chain configuration that brings the greatest economies of scale and scope.

In the majority of cases, companies endeavor to attain economies of scale within their existing value chain structure. They attempt to bring about a dramatic increase in scale in one or more of the links in their value chain. In recent years, firms have therefore tended to base most of their external growth on acquiring and integrating other companies operating in the same part of the value chain. This is known as horizontal integration.

With vertical integration, on the other hand, companies extend their value chain by taking on additional activities in upstream or downstream areas. A common aim in doing so is to safeguard supply sources or distribution channels. Equally, economies of scope can arise if the new value chain activities also make use of the existing administrative functions, thereby spreading the fixed costs of these functions over a broader base.

The capabilities of today's information and communication technology go much further than simply enabling companies to grow in size internally. Nowadays, firms can outsource services without giving up control of their value chain. Professional outsourcing providers can achieve economies of scale that the companies they work for would be hard-pressed to accomplish. For instance, a large partner working within a network could bundle administrative activities and free the smaller partners from the burden of administration. So vertical or horizontal disintegration does not mean giving up the prospect of economies of scale or scope. Far from it. It offers firms the chance to participate in other companies' economies.

Finding the Right Regional Expansion Strategy

Often the goals of low transaction costs and growth through regional expansion are mutually exclusive:

- Limiting business activities to one region keeps complexity – and the danger of diseconomies of scale – to a minimum. However, a strong regional focus also limits the growth potential. This, in turn, prevents economies of scale and scope from being exploited to the full by precluding, for instance, the exploitation of bulk-buying economies on the purchasing side.

- With geographical expansion, on the other hand, the risk increases that the economies of scale and scope will be eaten up by the high complexity costs. But expansion or even globalization can go a long way to increasing efficiency levels. When companies globalize their business activities, they penetrate a global sales market and new customers. This can also help them optimize their value chain: through global sourcing, for example, or global brand development, by manufacturing in countries where cost structures are better, or even by moving their R&D operations to wherever the best knowledge infrastructure is available.

The expansion strategy needs to strike a balance between, on the one hand, the increased costs and complexity it generates and, on the other, the economies of scale and growth advantages that is may offer. And companies should not forget that expansion is usually dogged by risks: growth scenarios should therefore take into account the possibility of partial or complete failure. However, the important thing nowadays is that sales prospects and production prospects are considered together – in addition to expanding sales, global expansion makes it possible to achieve new cost positions.

Optimizing the Product/Market Portfolio

The third dimension for achieving economies of scale and scope is the product/market portfolio. Ansoff's matrix identifies four strategies for exploiting growth potential (see Figure 13).

MARKETS / PRODUCTS	Present	New
Present	Market penetration	Market development
New	Product development	Diversification

Fig. 13: Ansoff's product/market matrix

Ansoff's matrix looks at the products a company offers and at the markets in which it operates. On each side, the matrix distinguishes between old ("present") and new. From this we can derive four strategies, each of which can deliver positive scale and synergy effects:

- Existing product, existing market: Here the aim is to generate growth and hence economies of scale and scope out of the existing business system or service spectrum. Typical operational levers include new branding and marketing activities (such as relaunches, brand profiling), pricing activities, introducing CRM systems, optimizing existing products and services, improving the sales organization and Sales-Up programs. Strategically, the focus is on introducing new rules, consolidating markets through mergers and acquisitions or establishing networks and cooperative arrangements. The goal is to better penetrate existing markets and customers. However, in view of the fact that markets are largely saturated and highly competitive, only incremental growth can usually be expected here – unless the M&A path is taken. The opportunity to exploit economies of scale and scope is therefore limited.

- Existing product, new market: The goal here is to take existing products and services into new markets, i.e. serving new groups of customers. The focus is on globalization. Operationally, this is achieved by establishing a local base, expanding the sales organization and entering into cooperative ventures. Strategically, mergers and acquisitions are a particularly good way of conquering new markets. Market expansion activities therefore overlap quite considerably with market penetration activities. However, growth opportunities are much greater – the potential economies of scale and scope are significantly higher.

- New product, existing market: This is the classic area for product innovation, with growth being achieved through developing and launching new products. Key here is a mastery of the three dimensions of speed, share and scope. This means launching the product on the market fast, quickly achieving significant market share through intelligent pricing and marketing, and thus realizing economies of scale faster than others (see also Chapter 1, p. 30).

- New product, new market: This entails diversification in the classic sense. Corporate growth is achieved by establishing new products or services that are not directly related to the existing product or service spectrum. Suitable levers include establishing new business segments independently, entering into joint ventures with venture capital firms for instance, or buying other companies. These levers can be motivated both by operational or strategic considerations. Diversification offers major opportunities for growth but it is also a risky business, as synergies with the core business are limited by definition. But they can be realized if the same strategic or business competencies apply.

Before we move on, it is worth stressing again that companies can achieve economies of scale and scope along all three dimensions discussed above – along the value chain, by choosing between regional concentration and expansion, and by focusing or diversifying. What position they choose to take within this will depend on their specific resources and skills, as well as the local conditions. And even when they have decided on a position it is by no means carved in stone: they should constantly examine where the greatest growth opportunities lie, and how these chances can be best exploited.

Diseconomies of Scale and Scope Put the Brakes on Growth

As we have shown in the previous section, economies of scale and scope cannot be taken for granted. They do not appear as if by magic. Companies must identify and exploit them through active management in both strategy and operations. They must also ensure that the economies outweigh the diseconomies – the disadvantages that inevitably accompany the growth process. In fact, companies are usually quite good at harvesting the benefits. Often there are experience-based management concepts for this. The problem for management is rather that controlling and reducing the diseconomies can place a massive strain on their time and resources.

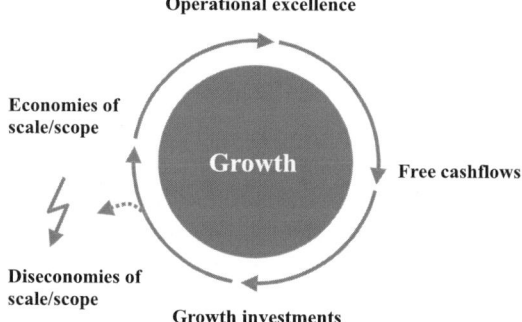

Fig. 14: Diseconomies of scale can disrupt the growth algorithm

Diseconomies of scale can occur at all stages of the value chain, including support activities such as finance, accounting, controlling and HR. Diseconomies of scale are what you get when unit costs rise as output increases. This can happen when machinery is operated in excess of its optimum level (internal diseconomies of scale) or when the above-mentioned geographical concentration leads to an excessive burden on the infrastructure (external diseconomies of scale), for example. Internal diseconomies of scale are caused by the increased complexity of large organizations. Diseconomies of scope occur primarily where the cultures of two merged companies are incompatible. Thus it is estimated that more than 50 % of mergers fail to achieve their growth and efficiency targets. But even internally driven growth can bring disadvantages that outweigh the economies of scale or scope, or prevent them from emerging in the first place.

The real danger that lies hidden in diseconomies of scale and scope is that they have the potential to disrupt the growth algorithm (see Figure 14). If the disadvantages of growth outweigh the advantages, companies find themselves forced to restrict their growth. This leads to the economies of scale and scope going unharvested. The benefits that come with growth are not fully tapped and so cannot be re-invested in raising operational excellence and achieving further growth.

This is the particular challenge of growth management: Companies must position the levers correctly so as to ensure that the benefits outweigh the disadvantages. Transaction costs play a key role here, as we discussed at the beginning of this section. And forecasts are unanimously predicting that transaction costs will continue fall. This is due in particular to rapid progress in information and communication technology (ICT): bandwidths are growing in all networks, data processing and memory systems are improving, and software is becoming better tailored to specific tasks.

In fact, it is primarily ICT that is keeping diseconomies of scale and scope within limits today. It allows companies to keep control of a large number of individual systems that can be structured so as to best reflect local market requirements. IT and telecommunications systems can make all the relevant data available in real time anywhere on the globe. And this is forming the basis of a new communications culture and changes in the mechanisms of management. Highly flexible ERP systems mean that managers can now call up any combination of performance indicators they want at the touch of a key. Intelligent, Web-based benchmarking systems improve the organization's learning curve fundamentally. Excellent knowledge management systems ensure that the company's accumulated knowledge is available throughout the organization and can be applied without coordination from the center. And ICT makes it possible for administrative tasks to be bundled and processed at practically anywhere on the globe.

Companies have an enormous potential to use the economies achieved by improved IT systems and the associated declining transaction costs to support both elements of the dual strategy of "restructuring and growth". First, they can significantly increase efficiency. If, as research seriously suggests, transaction costs account for between 50 and 70 % of value creation, then halving them will bring total costs down by at least a quarter. And second, the costs of transactions are falling both within and between companies. Companies therefore have a complete range of growth models to choose from:

- Internally, a company can grow without losing managerial control – powerful IT components simplify the necessary data flows and information exchange.

- External growth also becomes easier. Following a merger or acquisition, different IT systems often need to be linked up with each other, but this is a technical problem that is relatively easy to solve with the help of system integrators, for instance. Once the ICT platforms have been standardized or brought into line, it is much easier to integrate the merged or acquired companies today than in the past, when options for interaction between companies were much more limited. And once the communication is functioning properly, cultural differences can be overcome more quickly.

- Having a highly efficient IT and telecommunications infrastructure and compatible software solutions also makes growth via partnerships, alliances and networks easier. After all, it is here that information exchange between partners really counts. Overall, the market model is gaining in importance compared with the situation in the 1960s and 70s, when companies generally carried out all tasks in-house.

Companies must remember, however, that the combination of technological progress, falling logistics costs and political initiatives can shift the balance in favor of or against carrying out a task in-house or using an external service provider. An example: IT and communication technologies means that markets are becoming more transparent and it is easier for companies to identify suitable suppliers. With falling coordination costs, it can become desirable to outsource certain parts of the value chain, since production costs in the market are often lower than the costs of in-house production. This is because external suppliers can bundle demand from a number of companies and so achieve greater economies of scale than a company producing its own primary products. The result in this scenario is that the market's production cost advantage grows, the company outsources its production, and vertical disintegration takes place.

Of course, when we talk about externalizing growth we should not forget about the increased risk involved. Companies can reduce this risk by entering into long-term cooperative relationships with external partners: rather than continually searching for the ideal partner, they should aim for long-term relationships. At the same time, companies must weigh up the falling costs of security (and the longer term of the investments underlying the partnership) against the cost of searching for more advantageous or better relationships elsewhere. Long-term external relationships do have their advantages, but they tend to cancel out the crucial advantage of the market – which are more competition, and therefore more quality and/or better prices. And if the external partner turns out to be inflexible and so hampers growth, the company will soon suffer in terms of its competitiveness.

Yet, the fact remains: transparency-building IT and communications technologies and the removal of trade barriers are making it easier and easier for companies who are dissatisfied with their current transaction partners to find alternatives. This is putting suppliers under greater pressure to deliver good services, and thereby reducing risk. After all, inefficient transactions or those not contributing to growth can be selected and replaced with better ones.

Exploiting Growth Opportunities from Sinking Transaction Costs

What do sinking transaction costs and a diminishing transaction risk mean for the managers of companies? How can managers best exploit the opportunities for increased efficiency and growth? In the following sections, we suggest four tactics that managers can use to exploit falling transaction costs.

1. Actively Working Against Diseconomies of Scale

We mentioned earlier that diseconomies of scale generally come about when a company's transaction costs grow disproportionately as output goes up. Diseconomies of scale are more common in the case of internally driven growth, while growth through acquisition more usually results in diseconomies of scope. Here, the task is to reconcile the different structures, processes, systems and, most of all, cultures.

Today transaction costs have fallen across the board. This means that companies now have a better chance of growing without falling prey to diseconomies of scale and scope. In particular, it means that companies can grow large without managers losing their ability to control them.

But pain-free growth doesn't come automatically. Rather than sitting back and waiting for the economies of scale and scope to kick in, companies have to work actively against diseconomies of scale. Lower transaction costs represent the potential, but it's up to individual companies to exploit it. Companies must take action to avoid all three potential types of diseconomy – cultural, technical, and administrative. Below, we look at each of these in turn.

Cultural Diseconomies

Cultural diseconomies of scale and scope can occur on many levels:

- Loss of identification: Parts of the workforce in a highly specialized work environment may feel that their contribution is no longer relevant because its connection to the company's overall performance is no longer transparent.

- Breakdown of the corporate culture: The larger an organization is, the more difficult it is to create and live out a genuine corporate culture that everyone can identify with. Individual divisions and departments develop their own cultures, which may influence staff more strongly than the corporate culture itself. Similar problems often occur in post-merger integration, where peripheral values and objectives may contradict the overriding vision.

- Lack of innovative spirit: Innovations require both money *and* innovative spirit – in other words, a mindset that is open to new things. The crux of the matter is that while big companies may have the money to fund major innovation projects, they often lack the right kind of spirit to bring them about. This is the kind of innovative spirit usually found in smaller companies, which often have a distinct culture of risk taking and an unmistakable management commitment to innovation.

- Growing hierarchies: Growth often brings distinct hierarchies in its wake. In many cases, new departments are set up to assist in the organizational aspects of expansion but are not closed down when their job is done.

- Worsening communication: Excessively complex organizations often make communication difficult. Where there are too many sources of information, or where different sources provide conflicting information, the message loses clarity or becomes distorted. In such situations the office grapevine can sometimes become the only communication channel that is actually functioning properly.

Two steps can be taken against cultural diseconomies of scale and scope. The first is to make sure that the management of the company is both involved and trustworthy. The second is to employ an organizational structure in which the individual members of the workforce feel that their contribution is important to the success of their department and the company as a whole. The organizational structure must give staff the freedom to innovate. It should avoid multilayered hierarchies. And it must have clear communication channels for creating transparency. One such organizational structure is what we call the decentralized, trust-based organization. We discuss this in detail in Chapters 3 and 4. But it is worth noting here that the decentralized, trust-based organization is able to benefit so strongly from reduced transaction costs to a large extent because improved information and communication technology makes it so much easier to coordinate the decentralized elements. Companies that implement this organizational form are thus actively working against diseconomies of scale and scope.

Technical Diseconomies

Every company's technical infrastructure has certain optimum operating levels. Operating in excess of these levels causes costs to rise disproportionately: a piece of machinery working at the point of overload causes higher repair costs and raises energy consumption. What's more, fixed costs may skyrocket if production exceeds capacity to the extent that the only option is to invest in additional plant. In the short term at least, technical diseconomies of scale result. Technical diseconomies of scope result from incompatible technical infrastructure, a common problem if companies grow through mergers or acquisitions.

Technical diseconomies of scale and scope are easy to measure and relatively easy to ward off. Commissioning a new piece of machinery to increase capacity does cost money, but it is something that can usually be done quickly and without affecting the business processes, structure or culture. But technical progress also opens up new dimensions, allowing economies to be exploited and diseconomies avoided: a variable and modular infrastructure (machinery, IT networks) enables capacities to be increased flexibly and prevents fixed costs skyrocketing.

Administrative Diseconomies

The bigger the company, the greater the risk of administrative inefficiency. The chief reason for this is that internal bureaucracies have a tendency to grow faster than the company as a whole. Other causes are the reaction to legal requirements and the tendency for managers to make their own area of responsibility as secure as possible. The symptoms of too much administration include slower processes, increased complexity and growing inflexibility. Excessive administration clearly drives transaction costs, thus standing in the way of positive scale effects.

The restructuring efforts of recent years may have succeeded in identifying numerous cost drivers in administration and bringing them back down to an appropriate (that is, manageable) level. But we know from our consulting projects, for example, that many companies still have complicated and lengthy decision-making processes. Often the cause is complicated and all-encompassing systems of indicators – there are no simple metrics to channel the most important management processes in a sensible way.

Our recent analyses have found that too much administration can also substantially hamper customer relations. The "customer-driven organization" that almost every company professes to have appears to be little more than lip service. Turning it into a reality is a task that many companies still have before them: what are the needs of our customers? How do the different target groups want to be addressed and served? How should we channel their feedback so that all the relevant organizational units receive it? These are the questions that need to be answered if companies do not want to lose sight of the most important growth drivers. In the real world, though, this is often impeded by red tape.

Another problem is the different management approaches that often establish themselves in the different areas of a large corporation. This leads to inefficiency as a result of incompatible processes, systems and structures.

Recognizing that these diseconomies of scale and scope exist is usually half the battle. If top management dismantles these administrative barriers in a committed fashion, success can frequently be attained with relatively simple means. Methods include having clear responsibilities at all levels of the corporation, properly structured incentive systems and transparent and logical reporting systems. All of these actions are typical of what we call a decentralized, trust-based organization. They help keep transaction costs down, even in a large company.

2. Reconfiguring the Business System to Create Growth

With transaction costs sinking, differences in production costs are now even more significant than in the past. Suddenly it has become worthwhile transferring work from high-wage to low-wage countries, and to a much greater extent than before. The sharp rise in the amount of outsourcing to Eastern Europe, India and other countries with labor cost advantages shows that companies have recognized the potential of offshoring – outsourcing activities abroad – in particular.

Higher-value administrative services are particularly good candidates for outsourcing. This includes accounts and HR services, for example. Such activities do not belong to the core business of a company and so are less suitable for differentiation from the competition. What is more, they are often already bundled in corporate service centers. This makes them easy to outsource *en masse* with standardized interfaces with the rest of the company.

Europe is currently catching up with its competitors in the US in terms of offshoring services. This is borne out by the findings of a recent study carried out by Roland Berger Strategy Consultants in conjunction with UNCTAD. We interviewed 100 managers from a broad range of major European firms, representing more than 20% of the revenue of the top 500 companies. Our findings show that almost 40% of the companies already have experience with offshoring, and a further 44% are planning to offshore activities in the future. The focus of current and planned offshoring is back-office functions – higher-value administrative services, such as financing, bookkeeping, IT services and HR, as touched on above. These areas are chosen for offshoring by 57% of companies already offshoring activities and 64% of companies planning to do so in the future. One-quarter of companies planning to offshore activities in the future intend to offshore front-office functions, such as call-center services. A further one-quarter plans to offshore industry-specific services such as R&D. And about the same number use offshoring in multiple areas.

The key target regions for offshoring services are Asia and Europe. In 51% of cases, activities are offshored to Europe and in 37% of cases to Asia, primarily India. In terms of volume, the largest projects are found in Asia. Interestingly, the majority of offshoring projects within Europe have involved transferring activities to other Western European countries (29%), and fewer have gone to Eastern Europe (22%). This is certain to change in the future: the expansion of the European Union eastwards naturally creates new opportunities for companies to offshore activities to Eastern Europe. Geographically, the new member states are close to Western Europe. In terms of culture, they are much closer than India or China. Having joined the EU, they are now also better integrated with Western Europe in terms of politics and economics, and Western European companies therefore have a great opportunity to improve their competitiveness compared to US and Asian companies by means of offshoring to Eastern Europe. At the same time, Eastern European countries have highly-educated specialists who are generally fluent in one or more of the languages used in Western Europe, making them prime locations for offshoring higher-value services.

The most common argument in favor of offshoring is the reduction in labor costs (given by 70% of respondents) and other costs (59%). This is hardly surprising, given the enormous difference in cost levels (see Figure 15). And the companies we spoke to are already reaping the benefits: 12% have achieved cost savings of 10-19%, 44% are saving 20-29% of costs, 39% are saving 30-39%, and 5% are savings as much as 40-49% of costs.

Average labor costs, 2006 [EUR/hour]	
Norway	33.13
Germany	26.91
UK	21.10
France	20.37
United States	19.41
Spain	14.77
Czech Republic	7.92
Portugal	6.23
Poland	6.18
Hungary	6.03
Slovakia	5.24
China	1.08
India	0.95

Fig. 15: International comparison of labor costs (Source: Economist Intelligence Unit)

But the decision to offshore is not just motivated by costs: quality is also a factor. The quality question has two sides. On the one hand, potential quality problems are the number-one risk associated with offshoring according our survey. At the same time, many companies planning to offshore activities in the future actually hope to *improve* quality by means of offshoring. This was the case for 43% of such companies in the survey. And their hopes are not misplaced: one-third of companies who had carried out offshoring projects in the past reported that quality not only improved as expected after offshoring, but actually improved beyond the level of their expectations.

What do the new options for outsourcing mean for how companies manage growth? Companies now have the ideal opportunity to concentrate on their core business: their other activities can be taken care of by external service providers. Thanks to lower transaction costs and more powerful IT systems, management can remain in control despite the new interfaces that are created. And they can reinvest the money saved through outsourcing in the core business, thereby promoting further profitable growth.

Deciding which parts of the value to chain to keep in-house, and which to farm out to other companies or cooperation partners, is undoubtedly a strategic decision that should be made by the management board. Such decisions will become increasingly common in the coming years. We will see competition not just between locations in the home country and locations abroad, but also between different foreign locations. Such location decisions often have enormous investments hanging on them, and companies should consider them afresh each time. It is not enough for the board to make a once-and-for-all decision on the desired configuration of the value chain. Rather, top management must keep a constant eye out for new outsourcing options and decide whether the company should exploit them. Adaptability and flexibility are the key words here – which leads us on nicely to our next suggested tactic.

3. Increasing the Adaptability and Flexibility of the Strategy Process

Nowadays, structures that remain stable over the long term are almost unthinkable. The environment in which companies operate is changing too fast. Product life-cycles have shortened, customer behavior is changing more quickly than in the past, and new competitors are entering the market sooner. Opportunities for cooperation and outsourcing have increased. Lower transaction costs and risks mean that companies are less bound to one particular transaction partner. And standardized IT solutions make it easy to change quickly to a new transaction partner without incurring high switching costs.

In the past, companies could follow a particular strategy for up to ten years. Today, three to five years is more realistic. Plans that stretch beyond this become automatically suspect. This means that companies have to keep their organization suitably flexible. Accordingly, companies that use decentralized structures have distinct advantages over those that are centralized:

- Decentrally organized units are smaller and have leaner processes. This fact alone means that they are better at adapting to changes than larger, centrally organized companies.

- Because they act locally, decentralized units become aware of changes in overall conditions more quickly. They act like a seismograph, giving the company early warning of changes and so helping it to redefine its strategy in good time.

- Decentralized units act in a more entrepreneurial way – as long as their managers are responsible for their unit's profit and loss. Entrepreneurial spirit and flexibility go hand-in-hand.

A decentrally organized structure provides the overall framework for the company. We examine this type of structure in detail in Chapter 3. In addition, the strategic planning must take a number of success factors into account. These success factors – which we discuss below – make the strategic planning effective and help to keep the company on a growth track over the long term. They are all the more important given shorter planning horizons.

Modern Forecasting Instruments Give Early Warnings
Forecasting methods based on historical data (updates, projections, extrapolations) are no good for reflecting a rapidly changing business environment as described above. What companies need is a way of spotting the signals that would make them change track and adjust their strategic planning. They must see the signals before adverse developments lead to a crisis, and also before the competition is able to react and poach market share. Companies, then, need modern instruments for gathering and processing information – early warning systems, data mining, scenario analysis, game-theory models, options analysis, and such like. The benefits of early warning are obvious, especially with shorter planning horizons. Yet, in practice, companies still have a lot of catching up to do. As part of a multi-industry study, we asked 70 major German companies about the targets, methods and processes they used in their strategic planning. And what did we find? Only 30% use early warning systems.

Think Tanks Access the Company's Creative Potential
For early warning to be successful, models and analytical methods are not in themselves enough: they remain ineffective if staff don't know what to do with them. Management must therefore have the courage to set up think tanks, pooling the potential of particularly creative thinkers in the company. They should do this even in the face of resistance from the organization. For think tanks are often viewed critically, as their contributions are not reflected directly in the bottom line. Moreover, the ideas formulated by think tanks often venture beyond the accepted way of thinking – indeed, this is exactly where think tanks can be most useful. In setting them up, then, companies must ensure that they are truly free from day-to-day business and can concentrate on their real task of "thinking around" strategy. At the same time, think tanks should not be isolated from what is going on in the rest of the organization, formulating their ideas in an ivory tower. They have the vital ability to make the company's existing knowledge transparent and to integrate it with external knowledge. Any external knowledge that forecasts future developments that will effect the business is, of course, particularly inter-

esting for the company. Researching trends should thus be one of the think tank's essential tasks: trend scouts should gather information from the Internet and other sources, or hang out in the relevant milieu, sniffing out trends.

Decentralized Units Provide Valuable Input to Strategy Definition
Large parts of the company – if not the whole company – should be involved in developing strategy. In this way companies can make the best use of the knowledge accumulated internally. Nowadays, orders don't often come top down, especially in large companies. Instead there is increasingly close communication with the operational units. These units are to a large extent responsible for formulating strategy themselves, and they are given the necessary resources to do so. Where in the past companies would issue top-down targets centrally to the individual business units, they now integrate suggestions from the various decentralized units into a homogenous and focused overall company strategy.

Strategy Definition Is a Separate Activity
The strategy development process was formerly split between central functions acting independently of each other (Company Development, M&A, Controlling, etc.). This has now been replaced by an integrated model – Corporate Development. Corporate Development eliminates the artificial distinction between "strategy" and "strategic controlling." Strategy definition is now treated as a separate activity in itself, making it much more flexible. To meet the demands of speed and flexibility, strategic controlling and operational controlling must also be reorganized so that they occur at the same time. This allows Controlling to participate efficiently in strategy definition within the framework of Corporate Development.

Planning Corridors Allow Flexibility
Strict budget targets set by management restrict the employees' room to maneuver and stifle flexibility. What staff need are softer, more adjustable targets, such as planning corridors. Such targets are also a sign of the management's trust in its workforce, which pays dividends in terms of staff motivation. And this is precisely the planning approach taken by top-performing companies – as we will see in Chapter 4.

Employees Must View the Changes as Opportunities
It is vital that the employees view the changing situation as a challenge, and their new circumstances as opportunities. For this to happen, companies must prepare their employees to deal with the change. It is not enough to simply pass on responsibility to the staff: management must also provide the necessary tools for the job, otherwise the employees will quickly feel overstretched. This means more than just providing training in "hard skills" – it is also a question of changing mindsets. Staff must not see the rapid changes in their environment as a burden. Instead, the new situation should awake feelings of interest and curiosity. Of course, this can only happen if employees are properly informed about the strategy

and vision of the company, so that they have a chance to buy into it. And this means involving and motivating them early on in the change process.

Incentives Should Be Linked to Strategic Success

There is no doubt about it: Staff performance in implementing strategy must be rewarded in monetary terms. This is especially true today, with strategies placing heavier demands on employees and greater effort being required to implement them. Here, again, companies have some catching up to do. In our survey around one-third of managers reported difficulties in this area, often to do with connecting management and incentive systems to the strategic direction. Companies should therefore link staff pay to the strategic success of the company. And they should support their employees with targeted training and coaching.

Shorter Planning Horizons Require Closely Integrated Planning Processes

In successful companies the different planning processes – strategic planning, mid-term planning, operative planning – build upon each other. In the past, these processes differed noticeably in terms of their contents, level of detail, and time horizon. But with today's shorter time horizons, strategic planning now only stretches as far as mid-term planning. This makes it possible to interlock strategic planning with mid-term planning better than in the past. To do this successfully, complete clarity over responsibilities and interfaces is required. Particularly helpful are properly functioning communication between Corporate Development and Controlling, and standardized (or at least compatible) IT systems.

Implementation Controls Should Not Be Neglected

The number of companies systematically measuring the results of their strategic decisions is still too low. In our survey, only about one-third of companies said they did this in a professional manner, and just 20% used a balanced scorecard. Companies also fall short in their implementation controlling. Although the management board is often deluged with evaluations and analyses, there is often a distinct lack of reports focusing on the actual progress of the implementation. What companies need is quarterly reporting on target versus current status. The progress made in implementation can be kept transparent with the help of efficient action management and a standardized software basis for planning and controlling systems.

4. Reacting to Competition from Low-Wage Countries

Today's lower transaction costs mean that every company has the potential to reduce costs. Cheaper IT infrastructure, lower telephone charges and reduced shipping costs can be enjoyed by all. But this doesn't mean that competitive pressure is also falling. Far from it. In fact, competition is heating up as new players from low-wage countries enter the market.

Above, in the section "Reconfiguring the Business System," we looked at companies in low-wage countries taking over individual tasks, or even whole sections of the value chain, in outsourcing projects. But these low-wage countries also have companies operating in the same sections of the value chain as companies in high-wage countries. Previously, perhaps, they only operated in their home markets – the transaction costs in foreign markets were too high to allow an international engagement. But now that barrier is gone: transaction costs have sunk and these companies are free to start operating internationally.

Western industrialized countries are facing serious competition. Their low-wage rivals can now bring their low wage levels fully to bear. Sooner or later, their products will also catch up with those of Western companies in terms of quality. This, too, is thanks to lower transaction costs: today, know-how can be exchanged faster than ever before. Because disseminating information has become much cheaper and simpler, companies in low-wage countries can access advances in technology much more quickly. By the same token, it is easier for them to keep informed about the requirements of their foreign customers and adjust their product range accordingly.

So what can Western companies do? How can they maintain their lead in quality and product know-how? And how can they keep the discrepancy between their own production costs and those of producers in low-wage countries as small as possible? Four points are critically important:

- Don't stick your head in the sand: Nothing will be gained by rejecting cooperation and outsourcing agreements with companies in low-wage countries out of fear of know-how being transferred. First of all, this goes against the current trend in economic policy toward opening up markets, lowering customs duties and removing other barriers to trade – which, incidentally, is undoubtedly a positive trend. Moreover, Western companies have no choice but to exploit the low labor costs in low-wage countries. We have already seen above how lucrative it is for companies to offshore parts of their value chain. Any company turning their back on this is running the risk of becoming uncompetitive. But it is critical how companies handle their know-how: crucial expertise must remain firmly in the hands of the home company. This principle must underpin all contracts, processes and staff training.

- Maintain your lead in product innovation: Even if producers in low-wage countries catch up in terms of know-how, Western producers are still one step ahead in a large number of products. Companies must use their existing technological lead, as well as their lead in analysis and forecasting, to continue driving product innovations. Accordingly, R&D becomes of paramount importance.

- Keep production efficient by means of innovative processes: It is right for companies to exploit the wide differences between countries as far as labor costs are concerned, particularly in production. Contract manufacture in low-wage countries makes good business sense and is widespread. At the same time, production in high-wage countries still has an important role to play. One need look no further than the automotive industry or the IT sector – AMD producing the Opteron chip in Dresden, for example. Of course, production must be highly efficient to be competitive. Western companies must therefore make great efforts to employ innovative processes and to constantly develop.

- Use co-opetition: Companies can reduce competitive pressure by cooperating with competitors. This doesn't mean forming a cartel. It means cooperating in a particular market or part of the value chain, while remaining in competition in other markets or parts of the value chain. Co-opetition can range from developing joint standards (as with Symbian, a consortium of leading cellphone producers) to cooperation between banks over payment processing (e.g. Deutsche Bank and Dresdner Bank, who both use Postbank).

The picture should be clear by now: sinking transaction costs offer enormous opportunities for companies. It gives them greater room to maneuver and significantly increases their ability to grow. What is more, thanks to powerful information and communication technology, companies can grow large without losing managerial control. Yet, companies do not benefit automatically from sinking transaction costs. Management must actively exploit the possibilities. If they do this successfully, the self-perpetuating cycle of growth will kick in: economies of scale lead to efficiency gains, these then generate free cashflows that can be used for investments, and they bring further efficiency gains or growth spurts in their wake. In this way, companies can achieve the dual goal of growth and increased efficiency, as well as continually raising the value of the company.

The Decentralized, Trust-Based Organization

3. Decentralization – The Structural Basis for Profitable Growth

Summary:
We consider a decentralized organization to be the ideal framework for corporate growth. Its structures enable a company to react quickly and flexibly to changing demands in the market. Decentralized structures also have a positive effect on a company's growth culture – they form the ideal basis for entrepreneurial activity on the part of managers and staff. They also improve the conditions for transparency and communication, which are a major step on the way to building a culture of trust within the company. In designing their decentralized structures, companies should concentrate on exploiting the advantages of the new structure to the full. At the same time, they must watch out for possible harmful side-effects, such as the duplication of resources in different locations. One way to avoid this is to add certain elements of centralization to the decentralized structure. In other words, companies can steer a path to profitable growth by combining the best elements of decentralized and centralized models, tailoring them for their own needs.

Decentralized Organizational Structures Prevent Diseconomies of Scale

"If big is so damn good, then why is almost everyone big working overtime to emulate small?" Best-selling American author Tom Peters' provocative question hits the nail on the head. As we saw in the last chapter, a company can only achieve profitable growth if it fully exploits economies of scale while avoiding potential diseconomies. To do this – in answer to Peters' question – large companies have to try and capture some of the qualities usually associated with their smaller counterparts. Two qualities are key here: speed and flexibility. But emulating these qualities doesn't mean straying off the growth path. To take a Biblical example, David didn't beat Goliath *because* he was small. He beat him because Goliath relied on his size and didn't take his competitor seriously. So much so that he let his guard down. Goliath, the fighting machine, was not prepared for David's strategy: the stone from David's slingshot took him completely by surprise, and proved completely deadly. If Goliath had had brains, as well as brawn – plus some flexibility – David wouldn't have stood a chance. The moral for companies? If an organization wants to grow profitably in the long term, then it needs a structure in which the economies of scale (Goliath's strength) are not undermined by the diseconomies of scale (Goliath's inflexibility of mind and body).

Organizational structure plays a key role in avoiding diseconomies of scale. It is a crucial ingredient in preventing administrative and cultural diseconomies, or at least keeping them in check. Our international analyses and experience with companies bear this out: a decentralized structure, combined intelligently with elements of centralization, provides the best framework for successfully implementing the dual strategy of growth and raising efficiency. This chapter presents the evidence: we demonstrate why we consider decentralization the key concept for giving companies a structural framework for growth. To begin with, however, we examine the relationship between organizations and their environments, and look back at the history of how organizations have developed. After this we turn to the practical advantages of decentralized units. And we wrap the chapter up with some recommendations on how to structure a decentralized organization.

Structure Follows Strategy –
Organizations and Their Environments

You don't have to be an expert linguist to spot the connection between the words "organization" and "organism". They both contain the Greek root *organon*, meaning "tool". And their common etymological origin is probably not the only reason that organizations are often described as living organisms. In many studies of organizational theory, the organization is seen as a system in permanent exchange with its environment. This exchange is not one-way: it consists of a complex structure of relationships that operate in various directions. Thus, for example, changes in the environment will affect the structure of an organization, while changes in the organization will also provoke a response from the environment. In this section, we look at companies as a type of organization and try to discover by what processes of adjustment they react to new demands from their environment.

But let's stick with our analogy for a moment. Darwin's Theory of Evolution teaches us about the survival of the fittest. In order to survive, organisms adapt in response to changes in their surroundings, or change their environment to fit in with them. The same is true for organizations. In order to survive, a state of harmony must exist between an organization and its environment.

The problem is that environments are in a constant state of flux. This makes it impossible for companies to stick with fixed structures. The history of organizational models and theories provides plenty of evidence here. Markets, for example, are the key element in a company's environment. To a large extent, they determine the requirements of the company. So companies try to shape their production processes so that their output (i.e. their goods and services) reflects their customers' needs as closely as possible. At the same time, other elements in the company's environment – investors, suppliers, government, the public – also impact on its strategy, and hence its structure. Thus although to some extent the structure of the company has an effect on its strategy, the basic principle, as neatly formulated by Alfred Chandler in 1962, is that "structure follows strategy".

For evidence of this, we need look no further than how diversification and "divisionalization" have interacted historically. In the US, diversification began on a major scale after the First World War. Companies wanted to tap into synergies and at the same time balance out fluctuations in sales caused by seasonal or economic factors. To do this, more and more large companies started to expand their traditional areas of business. A classic and oft-cited example is DuPont. The company originally produced explosives, but expanded its product range to include paint, varnish and other chemical products. However, it soon became apparent that its traditional functional structure could not cope with this diversification. DuPont's structure collapsed. The reason, as Chandler shows, was that the company was no longer in command of its complex offering and was unable to manage resource allocation in its heterogeneous product portfolio. DuPont couldn't bring the crisis of coordination under control working within the confines of the framework of the company's functional structure. So it took what was, at the time, a radical decision. In the face of considerable opposition from within, DuPont decided to create five independent divisions for the main product categories, plus central functions such as Legal, R&D, Purchasing and Advertising. It was a bold approach – but it paid off: the reorganization was a complete success. As a result, many other diversified companies adopted the principle of divisional organization. And this approach also spread to European industrialized countries, albeit with a certain time-lag: the major wave of divisionalization hit Europe only after the Second World War.

Here's another example from the annals of history. It shows how different market conditions can influence the introduction and spread of particular organizational models. In the United States, the dawn of the twentieth century saw the industrial revolution in full swing. The introduction of assembly lines in the factories of major companies such as Westinghouse and Ford was turning production on its head and creating a quantum leap in productivity. This new phase of industrialization formed the background for Frederick Taylor's concept of scientific management, which he first published in 1911. The primary aim of scientific management – or "Taylorism", as it came to be known – was to increase the productivity of human labor by extreme division of labor. According to Taylor, in an efficient organizational structure, manual and mental work must be strictly separated and a system of regulation and control in place.

Taylorism soon came in for hefty criticism. Parceling jobs up into endlessly repeated minimal steps and depriving workers of any autonomy or stimulation was considered objectionable as it led to inhumane working conditions. Moreover, Taylor's approach ran the risk of systematically reducing the level of qualification of workers. But despite the objections, the concept found many followers – both in the US and the Soviet Union, which was pushing ahead with industrialization by any means possible in the 1920s and 30s. In fact, for Taylor's approach of extreme specialization to be successful, an enormous market for mass products was needed, coupled with large reservoirs of unqualified laborers. Not surprisingly, then, Taylor's ideas never caught on in Germany in their pure form. The state of the German economy after the First World War, where both capital and demand were in short supply, couldn't have been more different from that of the United States. Instead, Germany developed an environment in which highly qualified workers provided individually tailored services and products to customers.

Although Taylorism was hard to find in Germany in its pure form, certain elements of it did take root and even survived until relatively recently. Taylor's basic principles – specialization, the division of labor into planning and execution, a centralistic hierarchical principle of organization – have proved resilient in everyday business. Stable relationships in markets, product longevity and high productivity legitimized this type of organizational structure for industrial companies right up into the late 1970s. However, particularly in the 1970s and 80s, many German companies launched initiatives aimed at "humanizing the work environment". Their goal was to remove some of the negative elements of Taylor's legacy and correct excessive forms of specialization in production. The measures they introduced were essentially an attempt to move away from fragmented work processes and towards a more holistic approach. For example, the concept of "job enlargement" aims at reducing the horizontal division of labor by extending jobs to include identical or similar elements. "Job enrichment", on the other hand, aims to brings about a qualitative improvement in jobs by adding preliminary tasks and monitoring responsibilities. And "job rotation" allows employees to gain additional qualifications and avoid monotony.

Yet, despite such attempts at modernization, most companies' structures changed only gradually. The attempts at reform often led to the organizational structure being patched up here and there, while the centralized hierarchical principles and decision-making processes were left intact. How was this possible? Well, as long as the social and economic environment remained generally stable, companies could stick to their old structures without negative consequences on the part of the market. The two changed at the same snail's pace. How different from the situation today! The general environment for companies has evolved so fast, and changed so much, that organizations must adapt as they have never done before. This has called traditional structures into question and made many of them obsolete.

Speed and Flexibility – Survival Factors for Dynamic Markets

We have witnessed some momentous economic and social changes since the beginning of the 1990s, and in particular since the turn of the century. Of course, the world didn't change overnight. Yet many of us are only now beginning to realize the true extent of these ongoing processes of change. The transformation is being caused by a variety of independent factors. The globalization of capital markets and the markets for goods and products, coupled with rapid progress in ICT, have made competition fiercer and faster than ever before. As the complexity of the business environment has grown, the speed of reaction required from companies has also increased many times over. This, of course, is bad news for old-school organizational structures, which are unable to react adequately. To survive in today's competitive environment, a company must be able to adjust to change quickly and efficiently. It must constantly tailor its products and services to match its customers' needs. Speed and flexibility have thus become survival factors for companies – key competencies in today's dynamic markets. Organizations must adjust their structures so that they are able to meet these criteria. And there is one approach seems to do this best: decentralization.

When a company adopts a divisional structure, it is already taking the first step toward decentralization. In the past, however, companies tended to prefer larger units. As a result, a centralistic principle is sometimes encountered even within the divisions. More recently, pressure on companies to adapt to their environments has led to the emergence of a new trend. The question "how few divisions can we manage with?" has been replaced with "how small can we make the divisions?" In fact, there is no general rule when it comes to the ideal minimum or maximum size for units. The basic principle of decentralization is what counts, rather than exact figures. According to this principle, dividing a company into modules should have the effect of making its production of goods or services less complex, while improving its market proximity. Modular companies should be in a position to react more quickly and flexibly to customer demands, changes in the market and the behavior of competitors. Companies should bear in mind two principles when setting up their units (how the two are weighted will depend on the precise situation of the company):

- Process-orientation: Decentralized units should be tailored to fit processes. This keeps the number of organizational interfaces to a minimum during the production of goods or services.

- Customer-orientation: Customers play a crucial role in defining the requirements of goods or services, and thus also in shaping the production processes. This applies both to end-customers and internal customers (for services provided internally).

The Advantages of Decentralized Structures

We consider a decentralized organization to be the ideal structure for companies, since it allows them to react swiftly and flexibly to changes in their environment. Decentralization provides a framework that offers optimum conditions for corporate growth. And we're not the only ones who think so. As part of our study "Finding the Formula for Growth" we asked top managers what they considered the key success factors and preconditions for value-oriented growth. The majority agreed with us: a decentralized structure is an essential precondition for growth. Indeed, there are a whole series of reasons why decentralization has such a positive impact:

- *Market proximity:* Decentralized units are closer to the markets they serve, irrespective of whether they are organized along region, product or customer lines. This enables them to formulate their growth strategies in accordance with the specific needs of their own particular markets. Decentrally organized units also enjoy decision-making powers. This means that decisions can be taken locally, where the best information about the relevant market is available. This market proximity enables decentrally organized units to react swiftly and flexibly to changes in customer demands or competitive activity, adjusting their offering in line with local conditions.

- *Speed and flexibility:* Decentralized units are marked by short decision channels. In fact, not only is the decision-making process shorter and less complex, but the implementation of decisions is also quicker. This is chiefly because small units enjoy much better conditions for communication. Thus the number of communication partners is smaller, which promotes direct communication. Also, experience shows that the more levels of hierarchy there are, the greater the likelihood of information being lost or distorted. What is more, decentralized units generally have flat hierarchies, so there are fewer impediments in the information flow. The overall result is that decentralized units can act more flexibly than large ones, as both their structures and their processes are more compact. Adapting to changes in the business environment is therefore both quicker and less problematic.

- *Motivation*: Decentralized structures provide a perfect framework for increasing the intrinsic motivation of managers and staff. Why should this be so? Firstly, because decentralized units are usually responsible for specific processes. The staff of the unit see this process through from beginning to end, and this raises their level of identification. Secondly, in small, homogeneous units it is easier to motivate staff to work together than in the relatively anonymous work environment of a large company. In large organizations, by contrast, staff sometimes feel like very small cogs in the machinery of the company. This makes it much more difficult for them to feel motivated or to identify with the company.

- *Freedom and incentives:* Certainly, growth depends on innovation. But innovation only comes about when the conditions are right. It requires a good balance between freedom – even a certain amount of chaos – and specific timetables, priorities and budgets. And because the managers of decentralized units are closer to their employees than top management is, they are able to create the necessary degree of freedom more quickly and with less bureaucracy. This freedom allows staff to develop their creativity, which leads to innovation. Managers of decentralized units also have a better understanding than head office of what motivations their people need.

- *P&L responsibility:* Delegating the decision-making process allows the managers of decentralized units to act largely independently. This means that they become, as it were, entrepreneurs within the organization. They are responsible for the results of their decisions, both in a general sense and in terms of the actual profit and loss of the unit. This form of independence raises managers' motivation levels and unleashes their entrepreneurial potential – an effect that is even stronger if managers' pay is linked to their unit's performance. In order to delegate P&L responsibility, a decentralized structure is required. Decisions must have their cause and effect within the unit so that it is clear who is responsible for their success or failure. This means placing the decision-making process and competence firmly within the decentralized unit.

- *Freeing up top management capacity:* Decentralized structures mean that top management no longer has to deal with the day-to-day running of the company. Instead, they can concentrate on strategic issues. By contrast, if the organization is run centrally, questions relating to operations often land on the desk of top management. The result? Top management gets bogged down in the day-to-day running of the business, and strategic decisions are put on a back burner.

- *Transparency:* Decentralized structures are good for transparency both within the company and in its relationship with the outside world. Devolving responsibility for individual markets to different units gives top management an excellent overview of developments in these markets. This allows them to identify their high-growth and low-growth areas, and consequently manage growth through the structure of their business portfolio. Transparent organizational structures are also essential for accountability within the company. In companies with complex, matrix-like structures, it is often very difficult to pinpoint the responsible person when things go wrong.

- *Integration of other companies:* If a group is entirely reorganized, decentralized structures can prove very flexible. Decentralized units are relatively easy to regroup as they are generally responsible for complete processes, for example. Similarly, in a merger or acquisition scenario, it is easier to integrate individual modules; and in the event of portfolio streamlining, it is easier to dispose of a self-contained unit. So in general, decentralized companies demonstrate a high level of adaptability.

As Decentralized as Possible,
as Centralized as Necessary

In designing their decentralized structures, it is crucial that companies exploit the advantages of the new structure to the full. At the same time, they must consistently avoid potential disadvantages. The undesirable side effects of decentralization can include problems with coordination and the loss of a unified corporate culture. Another weak point in the decentralized approach is the tendency to use resources less efficiently than in a strictly centralized organization. This, of course, means simply throwing synergy effects away. As we have seen, decentralization is critical for embedding a focus on growth within the structure of the company. But if the management want to ensure that growth is profitable, they must strive toward a mix of both growth strategies and operational excellence. Simply ignoring the cost advantages from having certain functions organized centrally would therefore be highly counterproductive. The solution? Companies should add certain elements of centralization to their decentralized structures. In other words, to achieve profitable growth, companies should combine the best elements of decentralized and centralized models, tailoring them for their own needs. Based on our analyses and experience, we identify the following key factors for designing a successfully decentralized organization:

- The organizational structure depends on the business model employed. In other words, it is important to tailor the decentralized structure to the company's specific situation. Many different forms of decentralization are possible – from legally independent divisions to a holding company concept or an integrated network of closely linked business units, each with its own special resources and skills. There is no such thing as the ideal organizational form. Whether a company's top-level divisional organization is structured on the basis of product segments, regions or customer groups depends on the overall corporate strategy and on how well the different segments lend themselves to being split. A company pursuing a strategy of internationalization, for example, would be well advised to structure its activities along regional lines. Nevertheless, in the early stages of internationalization, it may be advantageous to house all international activities in one division to start with. However, companies must continually review their chosen organizational form and adapt it to subsequent changes in the strategy or business framework.

- Decentralization must be tangible in the divisions lower down the corporate structure in particular. The same applies to the devolved decision-making process. Motivation levels blossom if staff are allowed to assume responsibility for self-contained process steps within their direct sphere of work and get direct feedback on their performance. At the same time, decentralized units must be at least big enough to enable them to take responsibility for their own profit and loss.

- Decentralized divisions with specialist know-how that may be relevant to other business units or to the company in general should be set up as centers of excellence. This makes particular sense where a certain country has especially strong expertise in a particular area, such as the US in regard to product trends. Under the lead country concept, one country develops the corporation's marketing approach, for example, while another country handles purchasing activities and so on. This approach reflects the idea of integrated networks, but can also be transferred to divisional structures.

- The decentralized managers need to be integrated in the management of the overall company. This can be done by including them in a group executive committee, for instance. Top management benefits as they are kept directly informed of the status quo in the business units and can help steer them in the right direction if required. Divisional managers, for their part, are better able to see where their activities come in the overall strategic framework and may have the opportunist to influence corporate strategy.

- Decentralized units must focus on their core business activities, such as marketing, production or R&D. As far as possible, they should have their administrative functions taken away from them. Thanks to the outstanding levels of functionality provided by today's IT systems, bundling administrative functions in this way is quite feasible. But it requires an inevitable standardization of processes and systems. This can represent a mammoth task for companies that have gone down the decentralization road without a centralized point of coordination, as they often have a plethora of different software standards, organizational procedures, etc.

- In organizational terms, administrative functions are best incorporated in a corporate service center responsible for all the decentralized business units. From this starting point, service functions can then be outsourced wherever the market offers cheaper solutions for a service of the same quality. As we have seen in Chapter 2, nowadays this often boils down to offshoring. Service providers in different countries are now in a position to offer higher-value administrative services in areas such as HR or accounting, for example. In particular, the new EU countries in Eastern Europe represent attractive offshoring opportunities for Western European companies with great potential. A study carried out by Roland Berger Strategy Consultants in conjunction with UNCTAD found that companies can achieve considerable savings by means of service offshoring. In many cases, the quality of service also goes up. More than 80% of the European companies in our survey rated their offshoring projects as "successful" or "very successful", reporting cost reductions of between 20 and 40%. These savings come primarily from the greatly reduced transaction costs – a large part of what makes offshoring so attractive today. Thus communication costs are considerably lower than even a few years ago, making it possible for companies to exchange huge amounts of production data. Logistics costs and customs duties have also fallen significantly (see Figure 10 in Chapter 2).

Naturally, the optimum level of decentralization depends on the sector in which the company operates. Nevertheless, even in industries where the same, standardized products are available all over the world – for example, in fast food or entertainment electronics – it still makes sense for management to allow a degree of freedom at the local level, for example in designing and running regional media campaigns.

Decentralized Structures – The Basis for the Dual Strategy and a Trust-Based Organization

Before we move on, let's revisit two of the key messages of this book. Firstly, the dual strategy of growth and cost reduction. Decentralized structures support this dual strategy, because it's easier to manage the portfolio successfully in a decentralized organization. As well as acquiring and disposing of companies (or parts of companies), top management can instruct specific business units to focus on growth, while telling other units to concentrate on efficiency. Devolved profit and loss responsibility to the level of the units makes it relatively easy to see whether such a strategy is successful or not. By contrast, in a centralized company, resistance is only to be expected if one division is being asked to save money while another is hiring new staff.

Secondly, whether a company can carve out a profitable growth path, and then stick to it, depends on two things: its ability to grow, and its willingness to do so. These two factors rely on having the correct organizational structure in place. Our preferred structure – decentralized units with some centralized elements – makes an organization responsive and flexible. It also makes managers and staff act more like entrepreneurs, which has a positive impact on the corporate culture and therefore the company's willingness to grow. What is more, it improves the conditions for transparency and communication, and hence plays a crucial role in establishing a trust-based culture within the organization. And just what makes the concept of a trust-based organization such a powerful one, and how companies can implement it, is what we will be discussing in the next chapter.

4. The Trust-Based Organization – A New Management Model for Greater Growth and Efficiency

Summary:
Whether a company can carve out a profitable growth path and then manage this successfully depends on two things: its ability to grow and its willingness to do so. To be capable of growth, a company must have sufficient liquidity and appropriate structures. To be ready for growth, it must have the right culture. This means a culture where both managers and staff are motivated to use their skills to help achieve the organization's goals. The trust-based organization is the ideal medium in which to create this synthesis of ability and willingness to grow. It provides the perfect conditions for motivating – and mobilizing – the workforce to pursue the dual strategy of growth and increased efficiency. We present the strengths of this growth concept, its central areas of operation and the key levers for implementing it.

Trust Bridges Expectations and Reality

Trust represents a company's key growth capital. Companies face expectations on all sides. Customers want to be able to rely on the quality of the product or service. Investors expect good financial performance and proper risk analysis. Employees need to know their jobs are secure and that they are being treated fairly. Suppliers expect a stable relationship and prompt, accurate payment. And the economy in general expects long-term investment, environmentally sustainable production and tax revenues. Each of these stakeholders – and in reality there are many more, varying from company to company – has its own particular expectations, and its trust in the company depends on these expectations being met (see Figure 16). The company needs this trust: it is the foundation on which it transacts business, attracts investment capital, recruits motivated staff and forms solid relationships with suppliers.

72

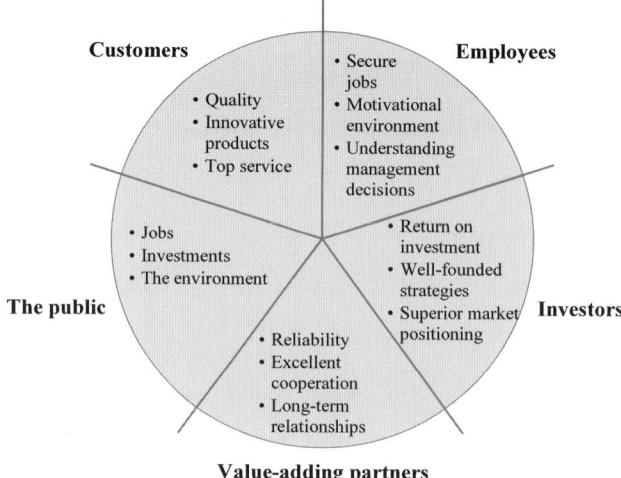

Fig. 16: Stakeholders in a trust-based organization

But trust, it seems, is just what is lacking. In recent years, the level of trust in companies has taken a severe knocking, whether from corporate scandals or simply as a result of poor service. Employees feel cheated by top management. Fat-cat salaries have come in for much criticism. Local communities no longer feel like partners with business, they feel held to ransom. A survey carried out in the spring of 2005 by the Gesellschaft für Konsumforschung revealed that only 32% of Europeans had faith in business managers. Only politicians are trusted even less (8%) (see Figure 36 in the chapter "The Macroeconomic Perspective"). In another survey carried out in Germany, 88% of employees complained about problems with their managers or ex-managers and 20% went as far as to say that they actually hated their boss. Equally alarmingly, a mere 12% of employed people in Germany described themselves as committed to their jobs. The rest, one presumes, are just putting in time (reported in the German weekly "Die Zeit", No. 45/2004).

Of course, the spectrum between trust and mistrust is very broad. A bounced check or cooked accounts (Enron, WorldCom and Parmalat spring to mind) are on a different scale to slightly disappointing service. A company choosing a poor communication strategy when it's in a tight spot is on a different level again. Yet, in today's society of open communication, all these negative cases can have a major impact. The media and Internet communities ensure that bad news reaches a global public, and in the process it often loses all sense of proportion. In the past, only a small group of experts took an interest in companies' performance figures. Today, they are pounced upon by consumer protection organizations and soon find their way into reports on flagging product quality. News travels at the speed of light and reaches the ears of all. The means and methods for transferring information have developed and grown, and with them peoples' expectations. Complaining about this state of affairs won't help companies: it's time to start adapting to the new environment.

What do we suggest? We believe that the best way companies can react to this new environment is to transform themselves into a trust-based organization. This is a management model that responds to the expectations placed on companies within a consistent overall scheme. And it has a whole series of practical advantages:

- It is not reactive. In other words, the model doesn't use up all its energy reacting in an uncoordinated way to individual trust issues as and when they emerge. Instead it is proactive, establishing a certain minimum standard that the company then communicates openly. This creates a basis of reliability in all the company's relationships.

- It takes a holistic approach to the problem of trust. The model's strength lies in the fact that it fully engages all the parties concerned. In so doing, it avoids the credibility problems sooner or later faced by companies taking a purely cosmetic or communication-based approach.

- It brings the whole organization closer to the goal of being ready for growth. Growth can only be achieved through trust, so the best approach is naturally for a company to focus on its own trustworthiness, and gear all its activities toward this.

However, the best thing about the trust-based organization is that, when a company starts acting with trust, it awakens the existing trust lying dormant in others. This trust solidifies into the basis for new, trust-building behavior. And so the process goes on, repeating itself over and over, the trust growing stronger and stronger. This is particularly useful because trust is not quantifiable: the amount of trust exchanged in interactions with the company cannot be precisely measured. Trust is more like the grease that enables the company's interactions with the market to run smoothly, an intentionally non-commercial element facilitating essentially commercial relationships. Naturally, this is part of the challenge: management often find it difficult to deal with this "soft", non-quantifiable factor. Indeed, they would prefer a more business-like set-up: "I place x amount of trust in you and expect y amount of trust in return". But one of the key insights of recent years has been that, when it comes to growth, it is not only the hard factors that count. What were previously thought of as soft factors turn out to be just as important in determining success as measurable indicators – indeed, often more important.

Of course, there is a problem. It is not possible for companies to "manage" the emotional aspects of trust directly. The task facing management is therefore to establish an organizational framework that fosters trust-based cooperation. But before we go on to look at how management can do this, let us examine more closely what the strengths of a trust-based organization actually are.

The Strengths of the Trust-Based Organization

Cultural aspects are crucial when it comes to implementing the parallel strategy of expansion and increased efficiency. Growth is primarily a question of having the right attitude on the part of both management and staff. If their mindset is such that they need to be dragged kicking and screaming toward the growth targets, then the company is never going to realize its true growth potential. Without a willingness to grow, there can be no growth. The willingness to grow must develop in the minds of the members of an organization, so companies need to create an environment in which employees feel motivated and qualified to pursue ambitious targets whole-heartedly. Such an environment is characterized by ambition, commitment and an enjoyment of competition, coupled with integrity and fairness: a culture like this will motivate employees to give their very best.

Fig. 17: Advantages of trust-based organizations

We consider a trust-based organization to be the ideal medium for nurturing a culture of growth. It is a model that addresses the specific interests of all the different external stakeholders at the same time, a holistic approach that aims to create a balanced synthesis of hard and soft factors. We identify four key advantages (see Figure 17):

- *Greater staff commitment:* Trust-based organizations enhance employee commitment. Staff want to know where their company is headed and how they are expected to contribute. Trust-based organizations create an atmosphere in which employees identify with their company. People who feel informed and included show greater commitment, are more prepared to learn new things and enjoy greater job satisfaction. What is more, they are prepared to go the extra mile when necessary. If people do not feel included in such a way, it follows that they have little motivation to do anything more than the bare minimum.

- *Better quality:* Believing in the readiness and ability of staff to perform pays off. This is a self-fulfilling prophecy: companies that trust their employees are generally not disappointed. Their positive attitude encourages and motivates the workforce, especially if this is backed up with appropriate incentive mechanisms. In this way, trust-based organizations encourage *better quality* of performance and thus *better quality* products. High quality levels are vital for success in the market, and trust is the best way to achieve and maintain them. Carrying out quality controls on the finished products at best identifies faults. Major advances in quality can only come about when staff are motivated to "live out" a quality idea.

- *Lower transaction costs:* Another advantage of trust is that less control and monitoring is required. Where agreements within the company and relationships between the company and its partners are based on trust, the organization benefits in terms of efficiency and cost. On the other hand, where the culture is one of mistrust, the company loses out on two resources that are in perennial short supply: time and money. In the environment is one of skepticism, a great deal of energy will be spent on safety mechanisms: endless paper trails documenting every decision, managers insisting on being cc'd on every staff email – the list of examples is endless. In a trust-based organization, by contrast, the decision-making process is often refreshingly fast and simple.

- *More innovative culture:* Trust-based organizations provide the perfect conditions for a culture of innovation (see also Chapter 5). Creativity can only be unleashed in a setting where people are able to formulate and contribute ideas in an open, direct exchange. This means not worrying that colleagues or bosses will take the credit for ideas, or reject them out of hand if they are the least bit unconventional. Trust is a vital precondition for knowledge transfer and management. Cultures of mistrust have an extremely counterproductive effect on companies' innovativeness, for which they are rightly criticized. Where companies experience a lack of innovative strength or flexibility, the reason often lies in their corporate culture.

In a nutshell, establishing a basis of trust can improve the entire organization in terms of both its internal and external relationships. It is arguably the single most important factor in inculcating willingness to grow in an organization. It also improves the organization's ability to identify and execute growth strategies. In other words, it integrates hard and soft factors. Managers, too, are aware of the positive effect of trustful relationships with staff. According to a survey of top managers that we carried out in the spring of 2004 and published in our study "Managing for Growth" (available in German only), employees consider good customer understanding to be the most important management factor. But they rate aspects such as a genuine corporate culture, a proactive information policy and management's physical presence right behind that factor. Below, we explain how a trust-based organization can be created. To do this, we examine its four key elements.

Creating an Organization Based on Trust

Trust is largely expressed through expectations. Is my business counterpart able and/or willing to meet his contractual obligations? Can the product I bought do what they said it can do? Can the company I'm investing in realize its strategy successfully? What happens to my career prospects if I confide in my boss about a conflict situation? Will my company implement the cost-cutting program as communicated, or are more jobs at risk?

Hence, trust grows if positive expectations are confirmed, but it grows even more if negative expectations do not materialize.

So how can companies establish this trust in its many manifestations? They can turn the intrinsic trust they are credited with in the early days of a relationship into genuine trust by proving themselves to be trustworthy. To achieve this, they need to be doing the right things, which means they must offer promising products and services. They also need to do things right, on two levels (see Figure 18):

- On a *personal and strategic level*: by fulfilling the expectations of stakeholders with regard to the people who hold management positions and control the future of the company. This is about trust in the ability of management to perform their duties and perform them fairly (personal trust). It is also about creating a sense of trust among the workforce that they will succeed in realizing their strategies and growth targets (strategic trust).

- On an *organizational level*: by fulfilling the expectations of stakeholders that, for instance, conflicts are resolved fairly, agreements and rules are adhered to, people are informed about developments quickly and comprehensively, and so on.

It is only when these two levels are given equal consideration that stakeholders are prepared to gradually translate the advance trust they granted a company into genuine trust. And it is at this point that the trust-based organization starts to live – and take effect.

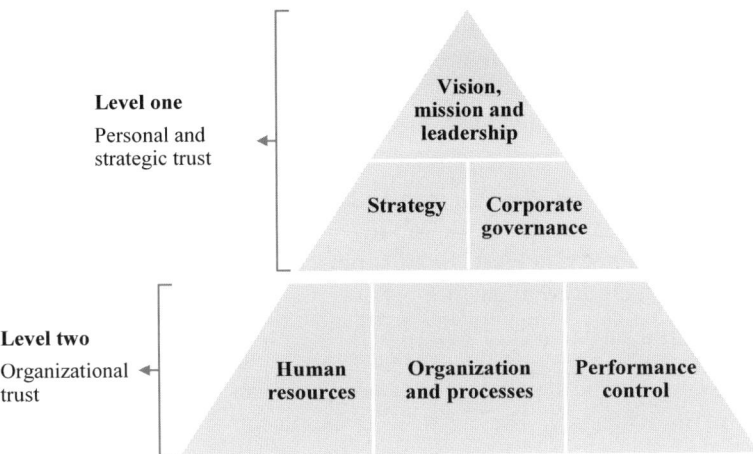

Fig. 18: The two levels of a trust-based organization

In Chapter 7 (Transforming for Growth – The Mobilizing Power of Change Management) we look in detail at how a company can transform itself into a trust-based organization. For now, we may consider the key elements that make up such an organization. They are:

- Excellent, performance-based leadership

- Decentralized organization

- Freedom to innovate

- Transparency

Excellent, Performance-Based Leadership

Leadership is key to the success of trust-based organizations. The deep, fundamental trust, not only of employees, but also of external partners and stakeholders, hinges on how management acts. It is the management's behavior that determines whether the organization is perceived as being based on trust or not.

The reason is obvious: people look to management for orientation, and what leaders do is taken to apply to the entire organization. Top managers epitomize what the organization stands for. This is why the company chooses precisely these people to represent it. And this goes for each level of the hierarchy, from team leader to board member – people always look to the next level in the chain of command. The fact that true leadership personalities are crucial to a company's success is also confirmed by the survey of top managers we quoted from above.

42% of respondents in this survey said that people were the key drivers of growth. This puts people ahead of competencies (process competency, relationship management, innovation) and systemic factors (strategy, efficient IT systems, brand management). The message? Without excellent leadership here can be no market success.

This makes it all the more important for managers to perform their role to the best of their abilities. Those who carry responsibility must be judged on whether the principles they live and practice meet the trust objective, and thus on whether or not they contribute to the growth objective.

Trustful leadership is marked by six criteria:

- *Strong credibility:* The credibility of a company can be measured by the behavior of its managers. They are the embodiment of everything that is good or bad about the firm. When it comes to credibility, the golden rule is, to paraphrase Friedmund Malik, "mean what you say, act accordingly and keep your promises." In other words, managers can only expect their staff to perform or behave as well as they do. This creates a basis of trust between managers and their staff that makes it easier for staff to accept management decisions and understand the rational arguments that lie behind them.

- *A fair, strictly performance-based approach with transparent criteria:* Performance-based leadership sets ambitious targets and clearly communicates how well they have been achieved. Companies must do more than give a performance-based approach lip service: the workforce must actually see it working in practice. Thus if employees use their professional competence and commitment to work toward the company's goals, they should be rewarded – including material rewards. They should also be able to observe and experience themselves that promotions are made on the basis of competence and performance alone, rather than favoritism.

- *Realistic but ambitious targets:* Targets that are too easy and targets that are too difficult have one thing in common: they're both motivation-killers. Naturally, this makes them ineffective as management instruments. In order to set realistic goals, management must first estimate accurately what staff are actually capable of achieving. On this basis they can then set "stretched goals" – targets that encourage employees' to be ambitious and encourage them to give their best performance.

- *Visible continuity:* The company's behavioral patterns and activities are based on defined values and a recognizable culture. This gives the workforce a clear framework on which to hang their own jobs and track their personal development. Continuity also helps staff understand the company's goals – a necessary precondition committing to them.

- *Individual support:* The management style must be empowering. Employees should be able to act independently, but they need individual support to be able to perform tasks and make decisions on their own. Giving them this freedom means that they can achieve the full extent of their potential and creativity.

- *Across-the-board involvement:* As far as possible, employees should be involved in all important decision-making processes. This is crucial if the culture of trust is actually going to come alive and start growing. Participation has demonstrably positive effects on levels of job satisfaction and motivation. The more say staff have in how the company develops, the stronger they identify with its goals. And participation leads to transparent decision-making processes in companies. Participation is thus critically important for building trust: there can be no secret cliques or old boys' networks that decide on the relevant strategic issues among themselves.

What is important for managers, especially in conflict situations, is always to remain authentic. As long as no one believes that infringements of the corporate principles will go unpunished, a solution can always be found, especially if the organization has a code of conduct for conflict resolution. Positively resolving a conflict can even serve to create trust because it demonstrates that rules and mechanisms exist and are taken seriously.

Physical presence is a vital aspect of trust. A company's executives can only motivate their people to contribute to growth if they are visible and accessible, and personally communicate their strategies and objectives. However, these kinds of communication processes also need something to actually be said – so they must have a clear growth objective and describe, in no uncertain terms, the steps involved in reaching it. Employees are quick to spot when the management itself doesn't really know where the company is headed. And that is when trust starts to crumble.

Target-setting also plays a crucial role in creating trust. The targets set by top management have a double impact: firstly on the company itself, and secondly on the outside world. For the company, they serve to motivate employees and are a measure of business performance. Clear top-down targets are required if staff are to assume personal responsibility for the results achieved. They also form the only basis for a fair system of incentives. For the outside world, targets and the degree to which they are achieved are an indication to investors, analysts and customers of just how the company is doing. Investors and analysts base their company ratings largely on how well they meet the targets they set for themselves. So even making a large profit can be disappointing if the company set its own targets higher still. This is not uncommon in practice, but it should never lead a company down the road of setting less ambitious targets in the hope of making a good impression on analysts when the results are finally announced. The workforce and its motivation level must always take precedence over analysts' ratings. Similarly, the chance that targets might not be achieved should not lead the company to announce one set of targets externally, and another more ambitious set internally.

Professional communication means having identical targets both internally and externally – as we will see later in this chapter in our discussion of transparency.

Special Feature: How Outperformers Lead – A Look Behind the Scenes

In the interviews we carried out as part of our study "Managing for Growth", we also asked questions about the best form of management. We wanted to know what instruments companies used, and what their experience with them was.

One tool that is used right across all different sectors is management by objectives (MbO). It became clear that companies achieving above-average performances evidently make better use of this technique. Indeed, 78% of the companies in our survey failed to achieve the targets they set themselves – a clear indication that something had gone awry in their target-setting process. The outperformers (those who achieved above-average profits and whose profits grew faster than their sales) had a number of traits in common as regards their handling of targets. We may assume that these common traits are much of the reason behind their success:

- Outperformers maintain flexibility by setting target ranges rather than fixed figures. Fixed targets such as exact budgets or precise sales figures run a greater risk of frustrating the workforce, as it is rarely possible to hit them dead on.

- The outperformers among the companies we surveyed set their targets along entrepreneurial lines rather than just focusing on numbers. Experience, will-ingness to take risks and creativity all play a part in their decisions, as well as the figures and analyses. For the managers of top-performing companies, then, intuition and understanding go hand in hand.

- Outperformers take the principles of the trust-based organization to heart. For example, they don't impose harsh sanctions if targets are not met. Even companies with above-average growth are not immune to occasional failure, but they take a different attitude toward it. In our survey, we found that companies who show outstanding growth in sales and profits impose much more moderate sanctions for non-achievement of targets than the majority of other companies we spoke to. The evidence thus supports the principles of the trust-based organization and argue convincingly in its favor: weak sanctions for missed targets have a positive influence on company performance.

Their success proves that the outperformers are getting it right: they achieve or exceed their growth targets, while other companies often fail to live up to their own expectations.

Decentralized Organization

As we saw in the last chapter, we must move away from the widely held principle that centralized organizations offer the greatest advantages. Trust-based organizations are the model of the future – and they require decentralized structures.

Inside a corporation, trust is built through direct contact between the employees themselves and between employees and their managers. Outside the firm, it arises through contact with the stakeholders. Obviously, such contact is easier and closer in companies with a decentralized organization than in large, centralized businesses: a culture of trust can be experienced more easily in small groups. Such groups also have the right conditions for realizing growth and operational excellence simultaneously: business units operating in close proximity to their markets know the needs of their customers in detail and can deploy resources optimally. Innovation is created locally. Information and decision channels are short and processes are more flexible and therefore easier to adapt to changes because they are more compact.

However, only companies that give their business units the necessary powers to look after their own affairs will become a force for growth. Those who sow trust will reap the rewards of growth. In this case, companies no longer use narrowly defined performance indicators to manage their business units, they use targets. How they achieve their targets is up to them. This allows them both freedom and performance-based pay – and both of these motivate the local management and workforce.

Decentralized structures promote growth providing they manage to sustain the cost advantages of centralization. The task is therefore to ensure the right mix of centralized and decentralized structural elements. Decentralized units should concentrate on their core business of marketing, sales, production or R&D; administrative functions should be consistently identified and brought together in corporate service centers wherever possible. If the market offers a cheaper option, internal services should be rigorously outsourced.

Where decentralized competence centers manage the core business, they need to be integrated on the basis of harmonized processes and structures. The managers of the decentralized units need to be involved in the process of corporate decision-making, for example by including them in an executive committee close to the board or another appropriate organizational unit attached high-up in the organization.

Freedom to Innovate

Innovation is the source of superior growth and returns. But how does a company set the creativity of its workforce free and channel it into products that are ready to market?

The answer is through freedom. Trust-based organizations create precisely this freedom. They promote curiosity and allow things to happen "by coincidence". They enable job rotation and thus encourage people to be flexible and think outside the box. In doing so, they help staff to enhance their skills and discover new things. They exchange their ideas with others whenever possible and delve into their concepts in greater detail, but they also measure themselves by what they have already achieved.

Our studies have found that the model of the "open space organization" is the most suitable for motivating employees to step out in new directions. The model combines freedom within a set of clearly defined responsibilities with rewards for success, which motivates staff to act as true entrepreneurs. By granting freedom, the open space organization creates the prerequisites for a culture of trust. Employees can truly *feel* that their company believes in their ability to achieve the targets set.

The concept of a open space organization comprises the following elements:

- *Clearly delimited roles and responsibilities* define the open space within which employees can act as entrepreneurs and innovators.

- *Flexible work arrangements* give employees or teams a relatively autonomous framework within which to perform.

- *Sufficient resources* that the employees can decide themselves how to use ("play money") allow them to use their freedom for experimentation.

- *An incentivizing compensation model* rewards the achievement of individual targets, innovative thinking and entrepreneurial spirit.

Regardless of whether or not a company adopts the open space organization model, trust-based organizations have three common objectives in terms of human resources management. The first goal of trust-based organizations is to empower and encourage their employees. This is done most successfully through a culture of participation, which ensures that employees are committed to the company vision and what it involves. In this kind of culture, it is easy to grant staff a certain free space within which they can be managed on the basis of their objectives. Secondly, trust-based organizations strive to make optimum use of their employees' capabilities. In doing so, they kill two birds with one stone: ensuring the best resource allocation and satisfying employees' career aspirations. Thirdly, human resources management is responsible for making the corporate strategy perceptible and therefore tangible to each and every member of staff, thus allowing all members of the workforce to understand exactly how they fit into the wheels of the great corporate machinery and contribute to the company's success.

Transparency

High-growth companies are always based on transparent organization, too, because transparency creates trust – and trust mobilizes all resources. A company shows its transparency in four main areas:

- Broadly embedded definition of strategies and targets

- Clear corporate governance

- Open feedback on performance

- Fast, comprehensive information on relevant occurrences

Joint *strategy and target definition*, more than any other corporate activity, is the best way to realize the fundamental factors of trust-based organizations, namely participation, transparency and clarity. However, companies will have problems maintaining a reputation as an organization based on trust if the vision is not lived out at as many levels of the organization as possible.

Trust-based organizations also tread new paths in terms of strategy definition. They develop their strategies in a process of exchange between decentralized and centralized business units, in other words they view their strategy process as a separate activity. They set a limited but clearly quantified number of targets. But above all they are aware of one thing: quality and content alone are not what make or break a strategy, but first and foremost how the strategy is embedded and lived within the company.

Recent studies demonstrate the crucial importance of internal communications in embedding a strategy in the company. Communication must be more than mere information. It must create acceptance, trust and commitment – through consistency, credibility and by speaking the target group's language. It serves as a point of orientation for the workforce and must create or intensify the internal pressure to take action. This is the only way management can get the new strategy incorporated into employees' personal system of goals and obtain their commitment to it. And this means that all internal motivators, opinion leaders and multipliers need to be involved. Choosing the right media mix to appeal to the target group helps ensure efficient and effective communication throughout the company.

Additional trust and commitment to the strategy emerge if the workforce sees that the company is monitoring how well the strategy is actually being realized and the intended results achieved. Many companies are not very good at this. As a result, new targets are met with resistance and employees become reluctant to work toward the goals, or even reject them altogether.

Many companies limit the monitoring of their results to earnings, profitability and efficiency targets. For example, what was the company's profit in month x? Or, how many cars were produced on day y? But when it comes to measuring the extent of strategy realization, this in itself is often hard to quantify. The controlling system must then rely in part on observations (such as the experiences of test shoppers), surveys (customer and employee surveys, for instance) and data from secondary sources (like market studies, benchmark analyses or external company rankings). Analyzing target deviations and deriving actions to correct them round off the tool kit for successful strategy monitoring.

Finally, it is critical that the organization maintain the trust it has worked so hard to earn when changes in the marketplace dictate a change in the long-term goals. Every strategic plan is subject to changes that need to be taken into account on an ongoing basis. But it is management's job to define the objectives reliably. Nevertheless, if changes are unavoidable, management must openly define and communicate the new targets. This is the only way it will be able to avoid giving the impression of having lost its way.

Good Governance Is the Best Way to Build Trust

Trust is established when an organization creates the impression that it is doing things right. *Clear corporate governance* is vital here, as it works in two ways to build trust:

- It *guarantees* trust: As a part of the system, it is involved in the process of building trust. The more reliably it functions, the greater people's trust in the organization will be.

- It *measures* trust: It sends out clear signals about how trustworthy the organization is.

The corporate governance system must therefore be transparent itself, and it must create transparency. It must define internal processes, set clear rules, determine the organization's competencies and stipulate the reporting channels. In so doing, it provides a reliable framework for all activities that it subsequently monitors and assesses constantly. This gives all stakeholders the security of knowing that their demands – in terms of fairness, information, the right of appeal, guaranteed quality levels, contractual compliance, and so on – are part of the system and are being taken care of properly.

This required transparency is once again a question of *open communication* and dialog between the company's top management and its stakeholders. In this day and age, companies see themselves confronted with countless demands for ethical behavior. Corporate governance is part of the response to these demands: companies that constantly check their own behavioral principles and their implementation against objective criteria avoid further public scrutiny. Secondly, they ensure that they are able to define their own mechanisms for building trust, rather than having to be measured against external parameters. In doing so, companies give themselves considerable room to maneuver in terms of how they become an organization based on trust. The very fact that trust is impossible to standardize, arising in specific situations only, is something that companies can use as a distinguishing factor.

As the starting point for winning trust, reliability also means clearly informing employees of what performance you want from them and giving honest feedback on what they do and do not achieve. Trust-based organizations are built on the fact that dealing openly with each other is the best means of building up reserves of trust. This also means informing people quickly and comprehensively about relevant occurrences. Today this is no longer merely good form, it can also be a matter of life and death for companies – in extraordinary situations like a corporate crisis or merger, for example. Depending on how closely they are affected, employees and external stakeholders should be told in an appropriate and honest manner about important incidents that occur. Companies that excel here win extra points in terms of trust. After all, when else is so much credit at stake? Three rules of behavior should be standard practice for corporate communication:

- *Parallel:* The company should speak the same language at all times – with employees and external parties alike (customers, capital markets, the media and so on). This requires coordination between the different internal groups: top management, press office, investor relations, the company magazine, etc.

- *Holistic:* Good information processes in extraordinary situations should consist of three distinct phases. The first phase communicates the decision-making processes that are currently under way or have just been concluded. At the same time it should already formulate new visions and values so that the workforce knows where the company is headed. The second phase focuses rather on communicating the progress and milestones achieved. The third phase is all about making the transition from extraordinary to "normal" situation truly felt. Staff must feel that their efforts have paid off and be motivated to not allow their performance to flag.

- *Professional:* In extraordinary situations, communication is a job for management. Piecemeal information or tactics designed to disguise the facts is something that will do lasting damage to a company's professional image. The truth counts if you want to hang on to key stakeholders such as high performers or investors. Demonstrating trust pays off. It is also important to let the workforce have their say, for instance through employee surveys.

Morality in the Company

A decentralized organization and a trust-based corporate culture to a certain extent depend on each other. Having a decentralized structure provides a number of key advantages. Thus expertise is not concentrated in one place, but can be pooled as required. Close proximity to the customer becomes possible. And the company has a precise understanding of regional peculiarities in production and the specific features of local markets. A decentralized structure also devolves responsibility and is thus the best way to encourage people not to be afraid of taking risks or making their own decisions.

But how is it possible to run a multibranched organization like this without substantial friction losses? The answer is trust. Trust is the grease that keeps the organization running smoothly. In the preceding sections we looked at the elements required in a company that adopts a principle of trust. These elements all have an unmistakable qualitative component: they are all ultimately about *how* things are done. To create a trust-based organization, top management must first declare – in no uncertain terms – that a trust-based organization is what they want and is what they are fully committed to. Such an organization can only become effective if management takes the first step. It is up to them to make the initial deposit of trust, as it were, and show clearly that they reject the principle of mistrust. Only then will employees and external stakeholders also come on board. Indeed, once they are convinced, they will be happy to do. The trust-based organization is an attractive proposition because it adds a moral dimension to the world of business. Thus, alongside the purely economic principle crucial for a company's survival, the trust-based organization follows a social principle in the way people treat each other. Respect, common values, honesty and reliability are forces that give business-oriented actions an extra element of morality that makes them easier to commit to. Trust-based organizations thus move in an upwards spiral in which trust is permanently renewed and grows stronger and stronger. And it is this that creates the basis for an organization's willingness to grow.

Achieving the Willingness to Grow

5. Innovation – The Engine of Growth

Summary:
Innovation is one of the key levers that companies can use to realize a parallel strategy of growth and increased efficiency. But can a company learn to innovate? Yes and no. Although there is no guaranteed success formula, we do know what conditions are conducive to the innovation process. How much money is spent on R&D is not the only factor – the corporate culture is just as important. Innovation and the growth that comes with it will only flourish in an environment that promotes creativity on a broad basis. At the same time, this environment must offer employees clear strategic orientation. As we have seen, the trust-based organization offers a suitable framework for this by motivating the workforce to give their best while at the same time allowing them room to maneuver. Now, it is time to look at what should ideally come within this framework. In this chapter we suggest a series of measures that can help companies maintain and improve their innovation capability even in turbulent markets. This includes building internal elites and integrating them into the innovation process, and creating early warning systems for spotting market trends. It also includes establishing a knowledge management system focused primarily on the quality, rather than the quantity of information.

Innovation – The Growth Potential in the Black Box

Innovation is widely recognized as the single most important growth driver. New, improved, value-added products and services make a real impression on the market and help a company stand out from the competition. One common microeconomic indicator is the share of a company's products that are three or five years old in the company's total sales; this reveals the relationship between its level of innovation and its growth. Yet, no one really seems to know how innovation actually functions. It remains something of a black box: we know what goes in, we know what comes out, but what happens in-between is a mystery. Not so long ago the business world thought it had found the key: innovation management. But by and large, innovation management just led to the good innovators getting even better. So what is the answer? Can a company learn to innovate?

Surprisingly, the answer seems to be no – at least, not according to business historians. Europe has a long history of successfully developing basic technologies in areas such as nuclear fission, aviation and space travel, information processing (computers, fax machines) and the definition of what we now call the World Wide Web. But it is the Americans and Japanese who have reaped the commercial benefits of these inventions on the market. They have adapted the technologies to the needs of the market and made global growth industries out of them: military technology, computer software and hardware, e-commerce and so on. Only in a few areas, such as the aviation industry, have the Europeans been able to turn their innovation lead into a market advantage. It seems it's not so much coming up with the idea that counts, but what you do with it – how you apply it, turn it into products and services, and then market it. For innovation to be financially profitable, you need to combine having the idea with developing it into something people actually want to buy.

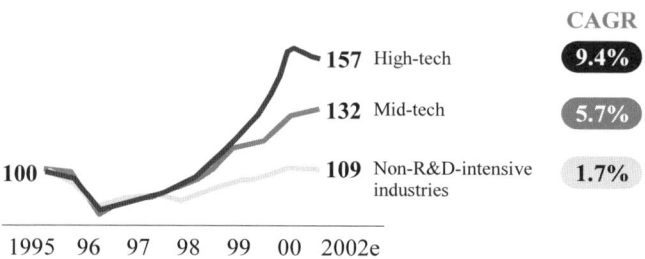

Fig. 19: Growth in technology sectors in Germany [1995 = 100] (Source: BMBF)

The facts and figures back this up. For many years, high-tech has been the fastest growing sector worldwide; we give the data for Germany above as an example (see Figure 19). High-tech is the most innovative part of any country's economy and requires the largest investment to be competitive. It also has the highest payback, as shown in Figure 20. Thus per capita growth in GDP is higher in countries whose industry focused more strongly on high-tech. The same is true for high-value services. Although innovation here is less a part of the mindset than in technology sectors, success in the service industry also requires a high level of investment in both continuous development and making breakthrough innovations. Analysis shows that investment banking, strategy consulting, high-performance medicine and innovative interaction-based services such as on-line auctions are major winners in terms of growth. They are also what are known as knowledge-intensive areas, i.e. they require strong intellectual input in the form of active innovation, especially since many high-level services have a strong technological element. Progress is only fast where innovative technology and innovative service combine and interact, such as in the field of logistics, where RFID (Radio Frequency Identification) and GPS are making new improved services possible.

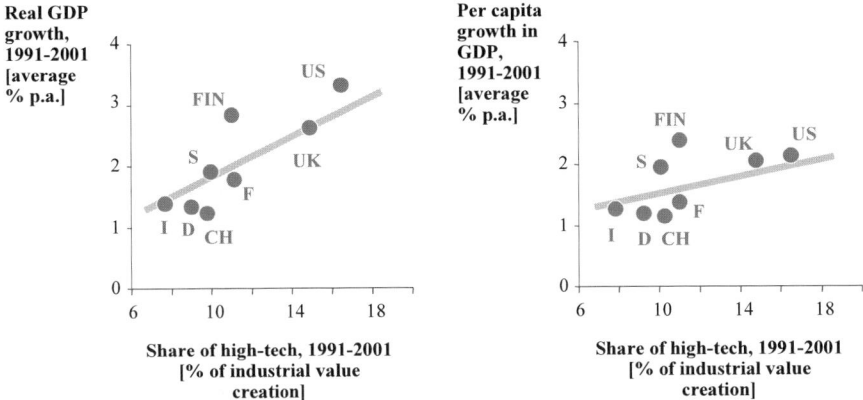

Fig. 20: Prosperity grows in proportion to high-tech (Source: OECD, own calculations)

Only when a technology segment reaches its saturation phase and the technology itself becomes a commodity, do its applications in R&D diminish. At this stage, however, growth rates also stagnate. The same goes for low-tech (or no-tech) industries: they, too, grow noticeably slower than industries where there is strong innovation. But companies should be careful not to jump to conclusions: what we have said relates to how the economy functions in general, not to the opportunities for individual players. Thus we find companies working with simple technologies who have outstanding growth stories. When we look closer, however, we find that in almost every case these success stories are based on innovative concepts (e.g. in marketing) or special services, that are likewise the result of development processes. It's not just the technological segment that determines whether you will grow or not: there are also examples of companies in the highest-tech areas failing to grow. As we said before, to achieve success in innovation, you need to combine two elements – having the idea, and finding the right place for it in the market. The true entrepreneur has mastered the art of defining and executing an optimum strategy for his own specific environment (technological segment, market/ competition, customers, suppliers, etc.).

This can also be shown by analyzing the relationship between the amount spent by companies on innovation and their growth in sales. We have carried out such an analysis for a number of companies working in the technology sector (see Figure 21). The results are clear: the more a company invested in R&D, the more successful it was on the market.

92

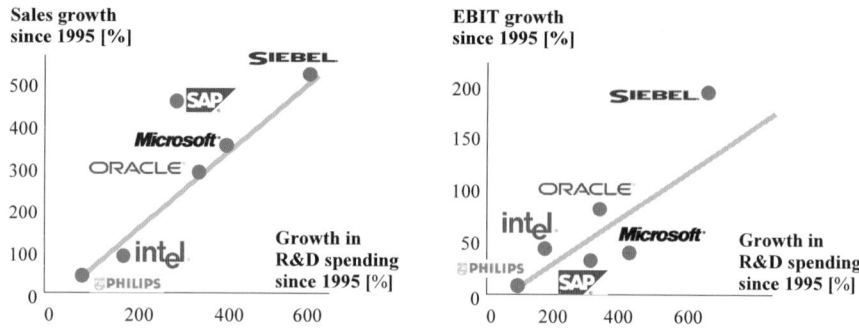

Fig. 21: Correlation between R&D spend and sales/EBIT

So, to be strong in innovation, a company must reach deep into its pockets. But that's not all. Innovation also needs the right environment. This is not something that can be prescribed from on high: it has to develop over time. However, once it is in place, it opens the floodgates for creativity. There is no simple recipe for making this happen: companies must find their own solutions and implement them with care and patience. The right culture for innovation is one that allows freedom, looks at results rather than actions and encourages staff to think out of the box. And such a culture is an essential part of the trust-based organization.

Innovation – More than Just New Products

When companies think about innovation, they often concentrate on innovations in products and services. In fact, this is only part of the picture. Broad-based innovation covers five areas:

- *Products and services,* i.e. extending or further developing existing products, or entire product ranges and new services. This is what is traditionally understood by innovation. However, this area also includes innovations that increase the value of the product for the customer, for example a new type of packaging that makes the product easier to use. Product innovations are the only way to generate new demand in a saturated market. Despite the risk of imitation, they offer significantly longer-lasting protection from the competition than price reductions and advertising.

- *Business model,* i.e. developing the way in which the company arranges its services into value-creating processes and ultimately offers them to the market. Innovation may occur in a number of strategic areas: the definition of the relevant market, the creation of customer benefits, the effective distribution of value-creation behind the scenes, marketing, the profit mechanism, etc.

- *Processes*, i.e. continuously improving production through the targeted use of technological and organizational advances (network building, outsourcing, etc.). Process innovations lead to better quality products being produced more efficiently, which is to say faster and less expensively. And because new products frequently require new processes, product innovation and process innovation often go hand in hand.

- *Supply chain*, i.e. the entire supply chain, from suppliers of raw materials and components right up to the end consumer. Unlike the process innovations described above, innovations in the supply chain include processes carried out by third parties. Innovations here concentrate on improving the cooperation between the company and its suppliers or dealers.

- *Customer care* refers to continuous efforts aimed at improving the way the customer is approached or supported. This can include developing new sales channels that allow the customer more flexible access to the company. Innovations in customer care also have a strategic element, as it is the market that decides whether they are successful or not. Innovations must meet customer needs better than what was on offer before – here, the customer perspective is important, not what the technical staff think of as progress.

Besides these five areas of innovation occurring within companies, there is also structural innovation that takes place in the economy as a whole. In the West, this means the shift from strongly manufacturing-based economies to increasingly service-based economies. This shift is the result of successful innovation in the five areas above. In other words, the prerequisite is creative entrepreneurs who introduce innovations onto the market as a result of their developments and willingness to take risks. Fundamental structural changes in a country's economy can quickly create great buoyancy: for example, one of the ways Finland managed to overcome the economic crisis that began in the early 1990s was to start investing strongly in research. And even in developing countries we find strong regions of growth where extensive innovation structures are being built.

Innovations don't always have to be radical. In all of the areas listed above, innovations are more often the result of painstaking work on the detail, or a creative reshuffle of existing elements. Innovation sometimes has an almost mystical aura surrounding it, as if everyone is waiting for The Big Breakthrough. Yet, there is good money to be made from improving a product slowly but surely. Major innovations like the automobile, blood-clotting agents or the Internet come along once every couple of decades. In the periods in between, companies should concentrate on recognizing their customers' needs and coming up with the right products and services to meet them. Alternatively, they can try to "rewrite the rulebook", sweeping away existing patterns (product technologies, business models, processes, etc.) and replacing them with new ones. Growth-creating breakthroughs like this are found in all five areas of innovation. Here are just a few examples:

- Product innovations: MP3 players are replacing Walkmans, DVDs are replacing videos, and advanced materials are taking the place of traditional ones.

- Business model: Application Service Providers (ASPs) provide software services to customers via the Internet, the customer paying for the amount of time used. This model is replacing traditional sale of software.

- Processes: RFID technology is currently being introduced in European and North American retailing, as well as between US government authorities and their suppliers, for example. This technology will make logistics processes faster and more efficient, and later form the basis for new types of retail offers.

- Supply chain: Efficient Consumer Response (ECR) in retailing improves the transfer of information at different interfaces, and so keeps fragmentation of the supply chain to a minimum.

- Customer care: With Customer Relationship Management (CRM), customer care is no longer limited to the purchasing process and selected after-sales services.

Innovations like these are hard to plan. They can be the result of years of R&D or simply a chance discovery. Even more than gradual innovations, they require a corporate culture that gives employees the space to be creative. In addition, companies must have the right people in place – individuals who are able to think out of the box. And this means that human resources, and especially recruiting, has a key role to play.

Innovation – The Key to Implementing the Parallel Strategy

Companies should innovate in all the five areas above. In so doing, they will be pursuing both strands of the parallel business strategy: generating growth opportunities while reducing costs. However, the immediate effects of innovation are quite different for the different areas. Successful product innovations, for example, have an immediate impact on corporate growth, allowing the company to reap the rewards of leading the field, at least until imitators come along. Process innovations and innovations in the supply chain, on the other hand, lead primarily to efficiency gains and cost savings. While business model innovations and innovations in customer care have a strong impact along both strategic dimensions. Thus a CRM system improves customer contact, generates additional purchases, and so brings growth, at the same time as reducing the cost of customer care.

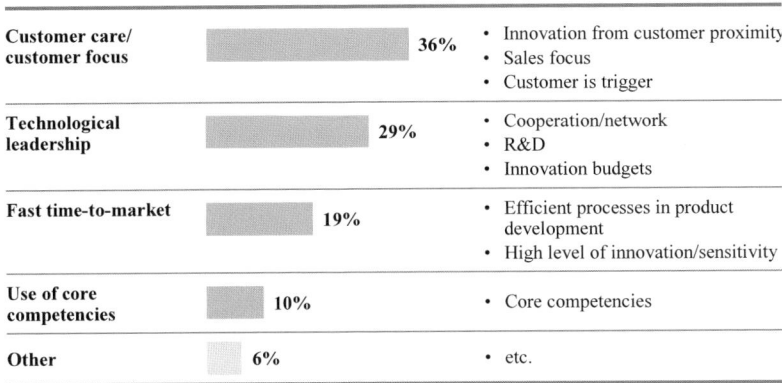

Customer care/ customer focus	36%	• Innovation from customer proximity • Sales focus • Customer is trigger
Technological leadership	29%	• Cooperation/network • R&D • Innovation budgets
Fast time-to-market	19%	• Efficient processes in product development • High level of innovation/sensitivity
Use of core competencies	10%	• Core competencies
Other	6%	• etc.

Fig. 22: Characteristics of the innovation strategy [% of respondents]

Via the growth algorithm (see p. 19 onwards in Chapter 1), all innovations support the dual strategy of growth and increased efficiency. As we have seen, the money saved through greater efficiency can be reinvested in growth. Innovations leading directly to growth usher in economies of scale, which likewise release funds that can be plowed back into more growth and efficiency gains.

However, a number of other factors also determine whether innovations can actually be translated into growth and increased efficiency:

1. Innovation must focus on the customer, since growth is generated by meeting customer needs. The respondents in our "Managing for Growth" survey confirmed this: for them, customer focus is the number one innovation strategy, rated higher than technological leadership or speed of innovation in terms of importance (see Figure 22). All five areas of innovation should therefore be geared ultimately toward the customer. For product innovations this should be self-evident, but it is also true for changes in the business model, for example. Innovations in this area will only bring growth if they increase the benefit to the customer: in Application Service Providing, for example, the customer only pays for what he actually uses, he doesn't have to look after the software, and he always gets the latest version. Companies must therefore anticipate customer needs. They should constantly be asking: What signals are customers sending out? Are there any signs that a change is needed? Are customers dissatisfied with the current product or service? Do they expect something more? Or are they over-served and now unwilling to pay for innovations? The answers to these questions will indicate the precise scope for innovation, i.e. the areas where developing innovations and investing money

will potentially bring a financial return. They will also provide a good basis for deciding what the balance should be between strategies focusing on cost and strategies focusing on growth. Of course, customer needs do not necessarily remain constant, and companies can change what customers want if they present a strong enough argument. This was the case with particle filters for diesel motors. German automakers failed to recognize the market, and accordingly invested very cautiously. They were subsequently taken by surprise by a French offensive that put particle filters right at the heart of the purchase argument – even for vehicles in the compact class – by appealing to customers' environmental consciences.

2. Innovation must take into account the maturity and saturation of the market in question. If it is nearing a point of commoditization, companies should adjust their innovation efforts accordingly: as Michael Porter says, it is time for them to decide between low cost (i.e. process optimizations aimed at reducing costs) and differentiation. Recent events in the mobile phone market are a case in point. Cell-phone manufacturers failed to carry out the necessary analyses of their markets, and the transition from boom market to overcapacity at the beginning of the new millennium took nearly all of them by surprise. The majority were still expecting growth and were acting accordingly. They then had to deal with the change to a buyer's market, in which differentiation was vital, in their innovation strategies.

	Outperformers	All companies
Innovations in customer care	57%	45%
Supply chain innovations	46%	47%
Process innovations	57%	44%
Business model innovations	50%	35%
Product innovations	36%	33%

Fig. 23: Share of fast followers in different areas of innovation

3. It is also possible to combine a cost and growth focus in a fast follower strategy. One of the surprising things revealed by our "Managing for Growth" survey was that the top performers in four out of the five areas of innovation were not always the first movers (i.e. those who were first onto the market with the innovation). More often, in fact, they were the fast followers (i.e. those who adapted quickly – see Figure 23). Fast followers achieve a balance between growth opportunities and costs by focusing on innovations that have already shown promise in market appraisals. Naturally, this strategy will not

work for every market. It also relies heavily on having a fast reaction time. Nevertheless, as our survey indicates, it can be followed with success.

The Basis of Successful Innovation

So, what can a company do to be a better innovator? To find out, we looked at some best-in-class companies and identified a number of common traits. These seem to be the essential characteristics for putting a company at the front of the pack in terms of innovation strength. And – managers, please take note! – the amount of money spent on innovation was not one of them.

Top of the list was a strong *culture of innovation*. To ensure creativity, top management must make it abundantly clear that they expect the workforce to put their full energy, both physical and intellectual, into innovation. This they must do for the sake of differentiation, competitiveness and securing the organization's future. The top management, for their part, should show their commitment to innovation by creating structures and introducing incentives (both financial and otherwise) to promote creativity. This can include job rotation, raising staff qualifications, forums for the exchange of ideas, efficient communication channels, comprehensive knowledge management and a strong competitive and performance orientation within the company.

As we have seen in Chapter 4, a trust-based organization is the best possible framework for establishing a culture that is open to innovation. It combines all the essential factors: empowering the workforce through communication and qualification, ensuring intellectual contributions and guaranteeing that they are recognized, and supporting individuals and rewarding their successes.

Many companies have completely restructured their organizations in order to achieve the right corporate culture. The aim here is to reduce the organizational barriers to innovation – such as highly formalized or excessively bureaucratic structures, a sharp division between those responsible for new inventions and those who will market them, top management being consulted too late on matters of strategic importance with regard to innovation, and such like. Put simply, creativity is only possible if the organization as a whole is innovative. The best conditions for creativity are actually small units with fast, efficient communication, direct transfer of knowledge and a detailed understanding of the relevant market. Companies that manage to recreate this garage-style, entrepreneurial atmosphere within a large organization have created the ideal basis for creativity. And here, again, the trust-based organization offers clear advantages.

Respondents in our "Managing for Growth" survey also mentioned a number of other characteristics typical of an innovation culture (see Figure 24). Here's what they said:

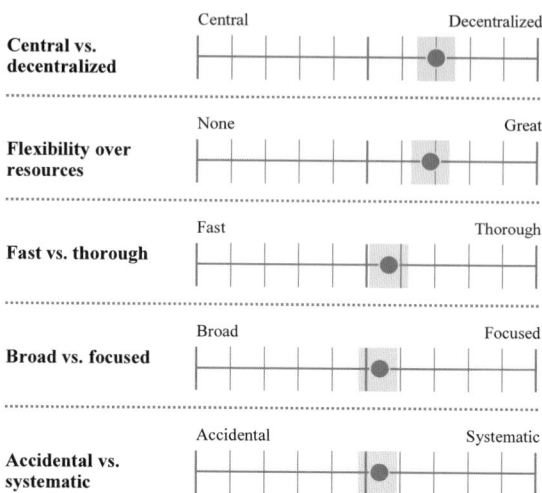

Fig. 24: How companies rate their own innovation culture

- In the decentralized units, creativity is focused strongly on the market. However, this is supplemented by clear guidance from headquarters regarding time lines, preferred projects, etc. This makes for an ideal combination of openness and a focus on results. Companies that take a backseat when it comes to managing innovation are not the most successful innovators, but rather those that formulate clear innovation targets and then "help the creative process along" with appropriate guidance. In fact, turning input into useful (i.e. growth-stimulating) results is a question of resource efficiency. Having no guidelines at all, or simply trusting that a market for the innovation will appear from somewhere, is a recipe for wasting time and energy.

- Companies tend to be flexible over resources. To be able to react to sudden changes in the market or cover the cost of unforeseen complications, a certain amount of financial elbow-room is required. However, if a company suddenly puts the brakes on costs at a late stage in the innovation process, it often loses all its previous investment.

- In the past, an innovation had to brake the mold – it was only worth looking at if it represented a quantum leap in terms of the product technology. The same went for services. Today, companies need only do as much as the market can support. Innovations should make the customer happier, not the engineer. The challenge is to find the best mix of thoroughness and speed to market (see Figure 25).

- Just as important is finding the right combination of breadth of vision and focus. Successful innovators follow a two-phase model: in the initial phase they are as open as possible, but once the decision has been made to develop a project and bring it to market they go for maximum focus. And to be able to make such decisions quickly and on a basis of facts, top management must be constantly physically present in the company and actively involved in all stages of the innovation process.

- Innovation processes are unusual, in that they do not follow a strict pattern or happen in a measurable or controllable way; indeed, sometimes they can be chaotic, bringing quite different results to what was expected (shown by the dimension "accidental vs. systematic" in Figure 24). Companies pursuing innovations sometimes have to stray off the familiar paths, and occasionally what seems like a detour brings them to their goal – although not always the one they thought they were heading for. Yet, leaving things entirely to chance is no good: companies should employ a targeted and systematic approach to achieve the best overall results.

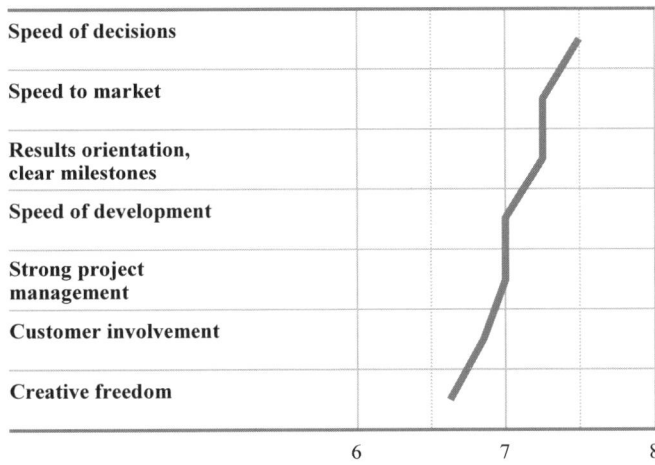

Speed of decisions			
Speed to market			
Results orientation, clear milestones			
Speed of development			
Strong project management			
Customer involvement			
Creative freedom			
	6	7	8

Fig. 25: Key growth drivers in the innovation process [10 = very strong driver, 1 = weak driver]

The Road Ahead:
Developing the Innovation Capability

Successful innovation was never exactly easy in the past – and it's going to get a lot more difficult in the future. There are a number of reasons for this. Competition in the area of creativity has increased enormously as the resources available for innovation have grown across the globe, especially outside the traditional intellectual centers of industrialized countries. Indeed, this is what the much-vaunted knowledge-intensive service economy is all about – the transfer of core value creation from "hand" to "head". In addition, the battle for funds has become much fiercer. Today more than ever, innovation must operate in an effective, cost-efficient manner. This is particularly true since the collapse of the e-economy. Companies are now less willing to invest in risky technology and increasingly expect to see tangible results.

Under such conditions it becomes particularly important for companies to continue to develop their innovation capability. This is the only way that they can still achieve successful innovation-based growth at minimum cost, in spite of rapidly changing business conditions and new risk structures. We have identified a number of measures that can help companies to do this:

- *Internal elites.* The concept of a "learning organization" is based on the belief that every employee in the company can potentially contribute to the process of innovation. This model works for most innovations. However, in addition to encouraging input from everyone, companies should build internal elites. These function internally as the drivers of innovation.

  Internal elites are the only way to guarantee that creative processes deliver business results. As many companies have already found, having a broad basis for input is ideal for gathering the best local information on markets, processes, customer expectations, technologies etc. But in order to channel this information in the direction of practicable innovations, companies have to synthesize the individual insights into a meaningful whole. This is where the internal elites come in. They steer the innovations in the right direction and put the individual pieces of the jigsaw together. The members of the elite are either generalists or networkers: they spot emerging trends and formulate them in such a way that others can then see exactly what innovations are needed.

  Incidentally, building elites doesn't mean creating special units separated off from the rest of the company. Elites only function properly when they are under constant pressure to prove their salt. For the best payback in terms of innovation, companies should ensure that the elites are open to newcomers and are working in competition with other groups; they should also continually be given new, ambitious assignments to carry out.

- *Early warning systems.* Today more than ever, timing is critical for success in innovation. Companies need ways of keeping an eye on what the markets and their competitors are up to. For this, a strategically planned and properly positioned early warning system is essential. The information it provides then needs to be evaluated. Internal think tanks and targeted market research are suitable instruments. Both of these must be in a position to provide top management with a solid basis for making decisions on the innovation course and the prioritization of current or planned activities.

  The information on market trends and competitor behavior supplied by bodies attached to the top management forms an important addition to the information provided by internal specialists, particularly in the area of product and process innovations. Internal specialists inevitably see the market from their own perspective. This is of course useful, but it ignores the bigger picture. Decision-makers therefore need their own information systems as a form of benchmarking against which they can judge the information they receive internally. They can also use these information systems to exert pressure on their own team if the competition is doing better. This is particularly important if the company is following a fast follower strategy, in which the use of resources is highly efficient as the company only invests in developments that have already been tested.

- *Knowledge management.* At the beginning of the 1990s, knowledge management became the boom category in management theory. It was suddenly discovered as the single most effective lever for management – as if managers had never known how to organize their knowledge before. Naturally, the new methods of information processing and communication it brought in opened up far-reaching possibilities. But the claims made for knowledge management went beyond what it could deliver, and the hype was inevitably followed by disappointment some ten years on. Since then, many ambitious knowledge management initiatives have been cut down to size and departments have lost their support and funding.

  This may turn out to have been a mistake. What existing, quantity-based knowledge management systems actually need is an added qualitative component. In the past, the obsession with knowledge management tended to create an information overload in which people were bombarded with often irrelevant information. Today, companies are discovering (or rediscovering) that the key is what you know – real, individual knowledge that can be accessed as and when required. It is not so important whether this knowledge is implicit or explicit, as was thought for a time. You can only be innovative if you have both specialist and general knowledge, and maintain and build on this. So, contrary to what was taught in the past, from the point of view of innovation capability it is not just a question of whether someone has fully mastered the methods of organizing his incomplete knowledge. Research ability and knowing the right tools are, of course, essential, but without real knowledge the key to their application is missing.

  Growth-oriented innovation management must therefore make a greater contribution than in the past to improving the quality of individual knowledge and channeling newly acquired knowledge toward the relevant part of the organization.

- *Partnerships.* Even innovations have their limits. In most cases, these are financial. After all, companies don't have endless resources to pump into new projects. The problem is that companies are often unable to predict which innovations are likely to be lucrative – i.e. generate profitable growth – and which not. This makes saying yea to one project, and nay to another, a risky business. One solution is to form partnerships with other companies, scientific institutions, specialist consultants and such like. We can see many examples where this has led to excellent results, particularly in the automobile industry, for example, where outsourcing R&D is very widespread.

Naturally, this touches at the heart of the debate about how much a company should share with others. The ability to innovate is often seen as a key strategic competence that should be kept within the company, for reasons of security. True, up to a point. But in today's markets, where the speed of innovation can mean success or failure, pragmatic solutions are called for if companies wish to participate in growth.

- *Racing yachts.* At the height of the e-economy boom, traditional large corporations were often criticized for being unable to create the necessary conditions for innovation. They lacked, it was argued, the necessary flexibility over job design, remuneration schemes with strong incentives, a fully competitive orientation, flat hierarchies and so on. At the time the talk was of "tankers versus racing yachts". This was the idea that big companies should set up separate units whose purpose was to come up with innovations. These high-pressure units should be run separately from the rest of the company so that cultural differences would not create problems between the parent company and its ambitious offspring.

  Since then, much has changed in the structures of major corporations. However, they have not been able to develop the garage-style entrepreneurial atmosphere we mentioned earlier. So it still makes a lot of sense for big companies to run innovation units where there is a high pressure on results (fast realization, competitive environment, creation of disruptive innovations, etc.) as separate units outside the main body of the company. Inflexibility on the part of the corporation is not the only rationale: it is also easier for small external units to talk to outsiders or even set up collaborative projects due to their physical proximity or appropriate positioning.

  Locating innovation units outside the company is not just good for realizing innovations, it can also protect the parent company from any potential shocks. New knowledge does not always extend a company's knowledge horizon in a beneficial way: sometimes it can upset the apple cart. If it challenges the accepted thinking too much, or makes a complete change of strategy necessary, it can actually endanger current market success. Separating traditional and new knowledge can prevent this happening and establish a basis for two separate growth strands.

Of course, whatever progress is made elsewhere, the eternal question facing innovators remains: what will ultimately be successful on the market and form the basis of the next growth surge? A market that does not yet exist, cannot be analyzed. It is therefore impossible to come up with a strategy for it – which is the key job of management – or find a way to capture it. And even in a market environment characterized by incremental innovations and stable relationships, it is difficult to estimate the impact of innovations. What should a company do if demand doesn't absorb the innovation because consumer habits are too staid, investments are protected, the price proves critical or customers fail to see the additional value?

Remember: innovating also means marketing. An innovation is only successful if it is accepted by the market, and this acceptance must be expressed in terms of actual demand. Praise from the pundits is all well and good, but praise alone will not make the company grow. Thus it is not enough for companies to bring innovation into the world, they must also provide it with a clear message that customers will understand. This is the key element in the innovation process, and one that companies ignore at their peril.

6. Identifying Cash Potential and Investing in Growth

Summary:
Growth must be financed either from external or internal sources. Today, with more and more barriers making external capital harder to come by, internal capital is becoming more and more important. Internal capital is a key success factor that determines whether the self-perpetuating cycle of growth can be set in motion: increased operational excellence generates free cashflows that can then be invested in growth. Growth leads to economies of scale that release more funds, which can in turn be invested in further improvements in efficiency – and so the cycle continues. In this chapter we discuss the enormous potential represented by sources of financing. This potential is currently undervalued and underexploited by many companies, as we found in our study "Cash for Growth". We show what changes companies need to make to their processes and structures in order to unlock the hidden cash reserves in their balance sheet. One key strategy is for companies to actively manage their receivables and payables, inventories and fixed assets. Optimizing value creation plays a central role here: companies can do this by designing a global footprint that is able to keep up with the dynamic development of global markets.

Avoiding Barriers to External Financing and Unlocking Sources of Internal Financing

As a general rule, companies have two options when it comes to financing growth. Either they can acquire funds from investors outside the company (external financing) or they can raise funds from within the company (internal financing). External financing itself takes two forms: either the company acquires new loan capital, or the owners increase the amount of funds they hold in the company (by reducing dividends or investing more equity).

However, both forms of external financing come up against difficulties. Let's look first at acquiring new loan capital. The behavior of banks has changed when it comes to making loans. Basel II has further tightened capital adequacy rules and as a result banks are compelled to adjust their loans to reflect more closely the level of risk represented by the borrower. The banking sector is also facing its own earnings problems and is under increasing pressure to consolidate. This leads to a situation in which banks are increasingly cautious about issuing loans, making it more difficult and expensive for companies to borrow capital.

But the growing costs – both obvious and hidden – of acquiring loan capital is only one of the factors that makes internal financing so important for companies. The growth algorithm points to another reason why it is worth companies identifying and exploiting internal sources of financing: raising operational excellence generates free cashflows, and these can then be invested in growth.

Essentially, there are two options for internal financing. Either you can raise your margins or capital turnover, or you can tap into your internal cash reserves by managing your receivables and payables, inventories and fixed assets. Given the fact that many markets today are saturated, there would appear to be little room for adjusting prices. Thus the option of increasing margins is rather limited, and the same is true for capital turnover.

The second option looks more promising. Hidden cash reserves have enormous potential, often neglected by companies in the past. There are four things that they can do to tap into this source of funding:

- Optimize accounts receivable management
- Extend payment terms for payables to suppliers
- Reduce stock availability
- Streamline fixed assets

Of course, unlocking these reserves requires a certain amount of effort on the part of the company itself. As with external financing, the company should not forget that management input is required to make the employment of capital more efficient. In addition, there is the cost of improving systems, such as purchasing more powerful controlling software. Despite this, the effect of taking the measures outlined above will be considerable: even minor improvements will reduce the need for external financing substantially. This fact was confirmed by our Europe-wide study "Cash for Growth", as we show below.

The "Cash for Growth" study was designed and run jointly by Roland Berger Strategy Consultants and the University of Lausanne. The study was carried out in fall 2003, with an update in fall 2004, and covered more than 200 listed Western European companies with sales of over EUR 1 billion. The companies came from 19 industries in seven industry clusters: automotive, chemicals & oil, consumer goods & retail, engineered products & high tech, telecom & IT, pharmaceuticals & medical devices, and utilities. Their joint sales amounted to EUR 2,900 billion – or roughly one-third of Europe's GDP – with an average EBIT ratio of 7.6%.

The investigation was based on publicly available company information as well as input from studies carried out by Roland Berger Strategy Consultants. It focused on those parts of the capital employed that are closely linked with the operational processes. We adjusted the traditional definition of capital employed by excluding non-operational balance-sheet items like goodwill, financial and intangible assets.

We identified an accumulated potential of almost EUR 420 billion in the companies investigated. This was potential that was simply lying fallow. The vast majority of it was to be found in the asset base, but inventories, receivables and payables also hid substantial cash reserves (see Figure 26). What is more, our research shows that the companies have not been able to tap this potential fully in the two years since the study. It is high time that companies started using these internal sources of financing.

Total potential [EUR bn]

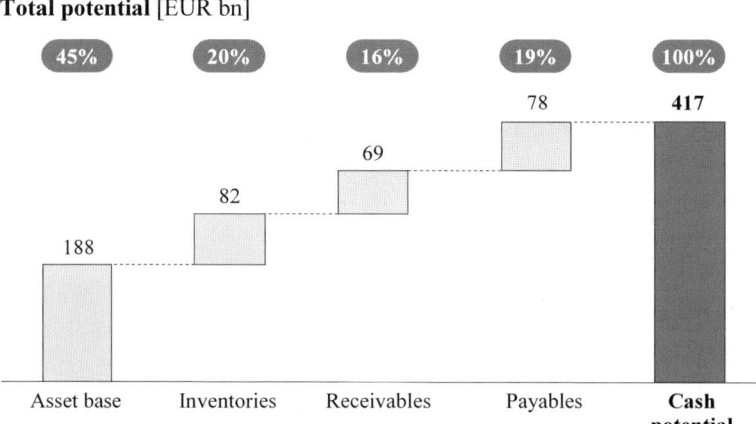

Fig. 26: Four internal sources of financing for growth [cumulative value in EUR billions]

A good indicator of how efficiently a company employs its capital is the ratio of operating capital to sales. This ratio is mainly influenced by the factors we have already looked at: net fixed assets, inventories, receivables from customers and debts to suppliers. In our study, the companies on average tied up 57 cents of operating capital for every euro of sales. And while the best companies used only 10 to 20% of their operating capital resources, the laggards in some industries tied up more than ten times as much (see Figure 27).

108

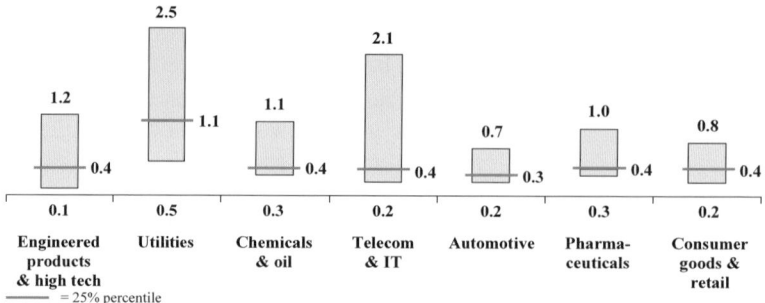

Fig. 27: Ratio of operating capital to sales by industry [1=100%]

Mining Unexploited Potential

So, how do the best companies manage to use so little operating capital? We have identified two levers that the leaders use to unlock hidden cash reserves. Firstly, they improve their relationships with suppliers and customers. Working together with these two groups, they increase the efficiency of their payment and logistics processes and so draw on the potential lying dormant in payables, receivables and inventories. Secondly, they optimize their production structures and thus streamline their asset base by taking advantage of local competitive advantages and adjusting their horizontal integration. Below, we look at each of these levers in turn.

Improving the Management of Business Relationships

The "Cash for Growth" study revealed an almost EUR 150 billion reserve lying unused in the short-term receivables and payables of the companies investigated. In addition, we found over EUR 80 billion in the area of value chain management caused by excessive inventory levels. This total potential is linked to less than optimal relationships between companies and their suppliers and customers.

Let's look at receivables and payables first. The best way companies can unleash cash reserves here is by employing a consistent value management strategy. This puts the cost of capital and refinancing right at the heart of the business activities: value is only created when the operating margin is greater than the cost of capital. Companies that focus on value management are thus particularly sensitive to cash reserves hidden in the relationships with customers and suppliers. In addition, there are a number of simple steps that a company can take to improve the management of receivables and payables. The following measures will have an immediate impact:

- Managing payment terms systematically

- Improving collection processes

- Introducing credit risk management to reduce the impact of payment defaults

- Placing responsibility for cash management firmly in the hands of the operational managers, who are much closer to customers and suppliers than the finance department.

Many industries have developed highly efficient processes for tight cash management along the whole value chain. Of course, some industries have less room for maneuver than others. For example, in the consumer goods industry there is relatively little potential for optimization, as the trading partners have enormous buyer power and can pretty much set whatever conditions they like. However, the general rule for companies should be to make managing receivables and payables a matter of the highest priority.

The cash potential lying dormant in the supply chain is somewhat smaller than that found in receivables and payables. However, at over EUR 80 billion, it is still a hefty sum. Supply chain management faces a basic problem: despite the spread of concepts such as efficient consumer response (ECR) and just-in-time (JIT), uncertainty over the supply process often leads to the build up of excessive inventories on both sides of the value chain, i.e. by both the supplier and the company. The solution is closer cooperation: the two sides should agree common targets so that they can both reduce the amount of capital bound up in stocks. This creates a win-win situation in which both parties can then get their hands on existing cash reserves. Of course, the prerequisite for this is an open trust-based relationship – an example of how the principles of the trust-based organization can have a knock-on effect on efficiency even beyond the company. The key elements for building the business relationship, as identified in our study, are as follows:

- Identify the benefits of close cooperation to all partners involved – in particular, that working on a basis of trust, rather than control, leads to lower transaction costs

- Set up a comprehensive approach involving all the business functions dealing with the supply chain, i.e. planning, procurement, production and finance

- Put one person in charge of all matters relating to a given business partner. The relationship includes both technical systems (such as a shared data pool) and agreements over personal cooperation, so identifying clear interfaces is crucial

Recently, several innovative concepts have emerged, such as collaborative engineering and collaborative planning. While they point in the right direction, the key challenge lies in rigorous implementation and a shared will to succeed. Many Internet platforms, for example, have come unstuck as a result of partners pulling in different directions or not fully committing to the project, despite their avowed intentions.

Optimizing Production Structures

One of the key operational levers to unlocking cash reserves is what is known as "asset productivity" or "asset effectiveness". This involves examining a company's assets critically to determine whether, and by how much, they raise the overall value of the company (assuming value-based corporate management). Such checks often reveal hidden cash reserves, particularly in fixed assets, which can then be unlocked by reducing the level of the assets. The "Cash for Growth" study identified a potential of almost EUR 190 billion here.

A company's ability to adapt its value creation to the demands of a globalized economy plays a key role in unlocking cash reserves. Customers and markets for industrial goods, for example, are increasingly moving to East Asia and Eastern Europe. Some locations in these growth regions have already caught up with Western Europe in terms of manufacturing quality and productivity. So companies have no choice but to redesign their global footprint. The basic rule here is to move each business function to the place that offers the best advantages in terms of efficiency, quality, know-how and market proximity. In other words, companies should bundle their resources in a worldwide network. In following this principle, they are implementing the precept of asset productivity and will release substantial cash reserves. However, this is not something that can be done overnight: designing a global footprint is part of a medium to long-term strategy. In a joint study with the Laboratory of Machine Tools and Production Engineering at RWTH Aachen University, we asked leading German industrial companies about their globalization strategies. They came up with five success factors for designing an ideal global footprint:

- *Optimize the entire value chain*
  Companies should re-examine their entire value chain. In the past, internationalization was mainly about shifting production to low-wage countries. But today things have moved on. Cost and efficiency gains are now possible right along the value chain – in design, purchasing, production and assembly. Outsourcing administrative tasks can also be worthwhile: there are companies in Eastern Europe offering high-quality specialist services in areas such as accounting, payroll and IT support, all at attractive rates.

- *Define core competencies, the future product portfolio and target markets in advance*
  The first task in planning the future global footprint is to clearly define the company's core competencies. The basic rule is that the company should co-ordinate all the stages of the value chain, but does not have to carry out every stage of the value chain itself. So it has to decide which key competencies are to remain within the company, and which are to be outsourced. Another central question in designing the global footprint is what customers the company is hoping to serve in the next five to ten years, and with what products?

And are key customers likely to shift their value creation to other geographies – in which the supply source should also change location?

- *Combine global planning with local expertise*
  Choosing the most suitable locations abroad is one of the most important keys to success. Management must first identify in which target location each business function can be performed most efficiently. One tried and tested method for this is using an evaluation filter, which companies can construct in line with their own specific requirements. As conditions in different geographical regions can vary widely, management would also be well-advised to work together with a competent local partner when choosing locations.

- *Evaluate global footprint scenarios in terms of potential risks and profits*
  Moving business functions is a risky business. It inevitably means disrupting established processes, organizational structures and supplier relations, all of which will have to be reconfigured in the new location. In some cases substantial investment will be required, to build a new physical infrastructure (buildings, telecommunications, IT) or hire and train new staff, for example. Outsourcing also has its price, in terms of the time and money spent looking for suitable partners and carrying out quality control. To avoid nasty surprises on the cost front, companies should first weigh up the total cost impact – the so-called Total Cost to Serve, or TCS – of the different global footprint scenarios. This provides a solid basis for deciding whether it really makes sense to relocate a particular business function or section of the value chain. A useful tool in the decision-making process is a risk sensitivity analysis. This can help determine the impact of changes in individual cost parameters on the overall cost structure. For example, what will happen to total costs if labor costs at a plant in Eastern Europe increase by 15% per annum? The next step is then for companies to evaluate the various global footprint scenarios from a financial point of view, ideally with the help of an IT-based simulation model.

- *Manage the process of transformation efficiently*
  A sizeable proportion of foreign undertakings – estimates put the figure at around one-third – fail, or do not bring the hoped-for benefits in terms of costs and efficiency. The reasons for this are complex, but most failures in global value chain design have their root causes in one of two areas: either the company lacks the necessary resources (e.g. experienced employees who are prepared to spend two years or so setting up the location abroad) or they underestimate the level of investment and time required to get a foreign location up and running.
  These are cardinal errors, but they can be avoided. Companies should remember that designing a global footprint is a matter for top management, needing their support and guidance. It is vital that they provide clear instruc-

112

tions as to what resources are to be used in each location and what share of value creation is to remain in Germany.

Top management must remember that designing a global footprint is not a one-off event. Reviewing international operations should be a fixed item on their agenda. Conditions in different markets are changing faster today than ever before. For example, countries that traditionally had low wages are attracting foreign companies, which is pushing up the demand for local workers and thus increasing wage levels. Accordingly, companies must constantly revisit their location decisions and adjust their global footprint as necessary.

Hidden Cash Reserves Are Found in All Industries

The hidden cash potential varies considerably from industry to industry, at levels of between 9 and 50% of operating capital. Despite this wide variation, all industries clearly have substantial potential. This is clear from the absolute figures for the seven industry clusters, presented in Figure 28.

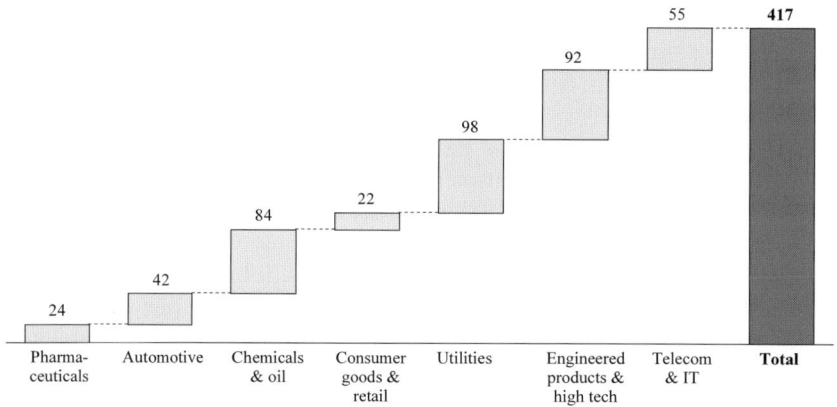

Fig. 28: Total potential of the industries examined [EUR billion]

Of course, identifying the cash reserves is only half the game. Whether a company can actually realize this hidden potential depends crucially on the ability of its management to create efficient processes and structures. Naturally, companies should not expect to be able to realize the full potential *immediately*, particularly in the case of cash reserves trapped in fixed assets. From our experience working with clients and interviews with experts, we would expect companies to be in a position to quickly realize about 10 to 30% of the cash potential contained in fixed assets. For inventories, we would expect about 50 to 60%, and for receivables and payables as much as 70 to 90%. This makes a total of EUR 240 billion for the companies best at implementation, i.e. just under 60% of the total short-term potential for financing growth. The average realization rate would be more conservative in practice.

To summarize, we believe that companies have enormous hidden internal cash reserves that they can unlock by actively managing receivables and payables, inventories and fixed assets. These cash reserves are, for a number of reasons, predestined to finance corporate expansion. Firstly, good business sense and the laws of competition dictate that such a massive potential should not be left untapped: if others act more quickly, the company will be left at a competitive disadvantage. Secondly, harnessing internal sources leads to lower costs for external financing. And finally, the increased efficiency needed to release the internal cash reserves is self-perpetuating within the growth algorithm: the funds released are used to finance growth, growth leads to economies of scale, and these economies of scale generate additional funds that can be invested in further growth and efficiency.

7. Transforming for Growth –
The Mobilizing Power of Change Management

Summary:
If top management want to put their company in pole position – and keep it there – they face a major challenge: they have to make the organization both willing and able to grow. They must inspire the workforce to give their very best so that the dual strategy of expansion and growth can become a reality. In practice, they often fail to achieve this lofty objective. Survey results show that there are significant barriers to growth within the corporate culture. These limitations can be removed by means of a change process that consciously manages the transformation of the company into a decentralized, trust-based organization, thereby unleashing its growth potential. The change management approaches of the past need to be expanded so that they make explicit reference to corporate strategy and encompass both elements of restructuring and elements that look to the future. Superficial or cosmetic changes are of no use: the goal is a process of change that ultimately leaves the company completely transformed. We present a model for this – the "4 Cs for change" – which brings together the essential elements for mobilizing the workforce.

Mobilizing the Workforce
Is the Key to Success

If one thing is clear from our discussion of the growth phenomenon so far, it is that whether a company is an outperformer, an average performer or an underperformer depends on the abilities of its top managers. Are they able to raise the growth potential in the company's culture and its structure, in other words to make the organization both willing and able to grow? Can they create the necessary conditions in which employees can realize their maximum creative and entrepreneurial potential? Are they able to turn operational excellence into a self-perpetuating growth mechanism? Do they have the ability to structure the dual strategy of increased efficiency and expansion in such a way that the team remains motivated? Or is the company at risk of losing its best people somewhere along the way because they can't see any future for themselves with the firm?

These are crucial questions, not least because most companies have a clear idea of what they expect of top management. Managers are also well aware of where their own problems lie: in the "Managing for Growth" survey, many were openly critical of themselves and their organizations. They are aware of how important people are as the engine behind change, yet they recognize that in their own organization practice does not match up to theory – whether in formulating a vision for the whole organization, motivating staff, defining and implementing quantitative targets or in their own personal proximity to customers (see Figure 3 in Chapter 1). Companies therefore have some catching up to do at the top, especially in areas of management that are important for growth: paradoxically, they appear to lack precisely those characteristics that are ranked most important here.

Our interviewees were surprisingly self-critical in other areas, too. Almost one-third cited cultural factors as the major barrier to corporate growth (see Figure 29).

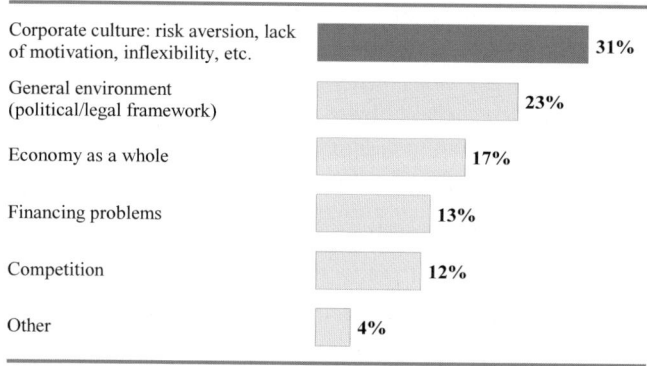

Fig. 29: Key barriers to growth within the companies

The survey also revealed the existence of an implementation gap as regards growth factors (see Figure 30). In particular:

- Decision-making structures are frequently unclear

- Customer understanding is often too weak

- A trust-based culture is not fully lived out

- Information is not passed on as early or proactively as it should be.

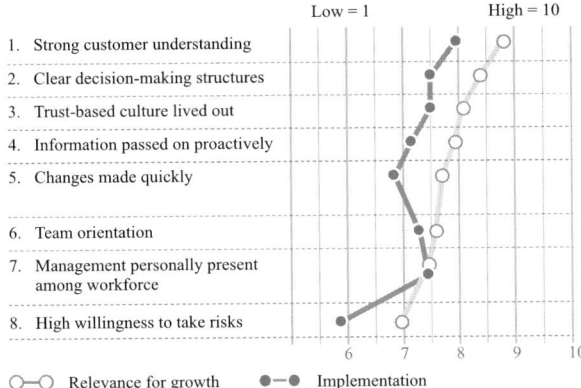

Fig. 30: The implementation gap for growth factors in the corporate culture

These questions of realization bring us on to the main subject of this chapter. Namely, what should the change process by which companies can overcome their limitations to growth actually look like? "Change management" is a term that often crops up in this context. The implication is that companies can consciously manage their transformation into organizations that are both willing and able to grow. This would certainly desirable – in practice, we find many examples of companies taking approaches that either come to nothing or fail to deliver the desired results. Of course, in some cases this is due to problems with the planning or execution, such as an overambitious time-plan, excessive complexity, the lack of an explicit goal that everyone can sign up to, or a belief in the infallibility of the plan. In many cases, however, the real problem lies elsewhere.

From our work with companies, we know of two major barriers to the change process. The first is inertia at top management level, not so much due to a conscious passivity, but rather the carefully wrought balance between different business functions, or between trade unions and management. Change of whatever sort risks upsetting this delicate balance, so it becomes preferable to put up with a suboptimal situation – especially if one can point to growth rates that are, although not outstanding, nonetheless solid. However, in this case, half of the dual aim of ability and willingness to grow is clearly missing. Moreover, if the management does initiate a change process solely in response to external (i.e. market) or internal, number-driven pressure, how can it hope to motivate the workforce to act and think in an independent, forward-looking manner?

The second barrier is that the whole concept of change has lost its edge in many companies today. Half-hearted, rushed or chaotic change programs, often abandoned halfway through, have over the course of many years undermined the willingness of staff to contribute to restructuring – a severe case of what is commonly known as change fatigue.

These observations lead us to a clear conclusion: it is not so much a new conceptual approach that is needed, as a different attitude toward the change process itself. The attitude toward the change process is what determines both its goals and the approach taken. And only if this attitude is right, does the process stand a chance of being successful.

This means that many of the change management approaches developed in the 1990s can essentially still be used. All that needs to be done is to add a couple of extra elements:

1. Ensure the change management approach makes explicit reference to corporate strategy.

2. Incorporate both elements of restructuring and elements that look to the future.

3. Introduce new measures and anchor these in the organization in such a way that the change process ultimately leaves the company internally transformed. The change must lead to a transformation that represents an explicit and conscious break with the past, involving the whole company.

What makes these extra elements so important? Well, the change process must be directed toward clear, unambiguous, analytically derived goals in order for the necessary for them to have the necessary "pull". Incidentally, the more broadly strategy definition can be anchored within the company, the more effective this lever will be. Involving staff in strategy definition makes them both committed and more willing to put up with the conflicts that arise. And that there will be conflicts is inevitable, since too much flexibility damages the strategy as a whole, along with its credibility.

This is particularly true since the strategy must achieve a balance between cost targets (operational excellence, business portfolio, etc.) and growth targets. The aim of the change management program, which is based on this strategy, is therefore to develop the company in the direction of both of these objectives at the same time. Thus the typical objection that the change program is just a cost-cutting exercise and lacks a long-term perspective, no longer applies.

The parallel strategy of growth and cost reduction is particularly important, as nowadays companies must be prepared to contract and expand at the same time or in rapid succession. This represents a particular challenge for management. The aim of the change process is therefore to prepare and motivate staff for two things. On the one hand, the workforce must sustain their efforts to raise productivity and efficiency. And at the same time they should see that top management has a long-term plan for corporate development, and that it wants and needs them to make a personal contribution to this.

We now come to the actual design of the change process. Here, it is worth remembering Kurt Lewin's change theory, which looks at the psychological aspects of change. Lewin identifies three clearly-defined stages of change that follow on from each other. The first stage is "unfreezing", in which the organization is deliberately opened up to the idea of change. The second stage is "changing", i.e. the actual implementation of the changes. And the final stage is "refreezing", a period of stabilization in which the change process is consciously and explicitly brought to completion.

Although Lewin's change model appears in all the standard textbooks, it is rarely lived out by companies in practice. Yet, intuitively, we know that during a process of change people need a fixed point of orientation, something that will help them regain their equilibrium at least temporarily. Lewin's model answers this in two ways. Firstly, in his ideal process, the transition from the original state of equilibrium to the state of change is consciously shaped, and not simply prescribed from on high. And secondly, the process ends with refreezing, in other words the creation of a new equilibrium. This is important because the goal of the transformation is not the abandoning of the old status or the process of change itself, but rather the new organization, changed for the better and now ready for new things. For the new organization to be accepted the management must give a clear signal that it represents the new state of equilibrium and thus the end of the process of change, with its inevitable insecurities. Thus if a company wants the workforce to join them on their journey of transformation, it is important that they also announce when the final destination has been reached. Failing to give the transformation a definitive end-point is just as damaging for acceptance as constantly extending the change processes or pushing back deadlines.

Lewin's model forms the backbone of the change process, supporting the individual components that make it up. Companies that want to turn themselves into trust-based organizations and thus put themselves onto a growth path would do well to note that the journey itself is the goal, not the final destination. The trust-based organization must deliver what it promises even while it is being created. This is all the more difficult since the transformation into trust-based organization represents a fundamental transformation and not just a series of improvements to existing processes. It must embrace both the way the company operates and its value system. Success in building a trust-based organization, measured in terms of acceptance, mobilization for growth, stimulation of innovation and so on, depends on top management being tangibly present in the organization and managing all the individual change processes according to a detailed action plan. Change projects are not something that can be delegated – you can't just fix an overall target and then put a project manager on the job. The company's employees need to see top management rolling up their sleeves and really getting involved, and top management must be around to deal with any questions and allay any concerns. The credibility of the entire change project depends on the direct involvement of the people at the top: after all, transformation represents the implementation of a business strategy, and if the managers take a back seat, the employees will think that they don't fully believe in the strategy. The quality of the top management shines through in a change process, both in terms of the behind-the-scenes planning and preparation and in their involvement in its implementation.

What are the implications of this? Firstly that change management requires more input in terms of time and energy than many managers would like to believe. They have to try and find a middle path between two extremes – getting bogged down in the detail is just as unhelpful as standing on the sidelines and refusing to get their hands dirty. Top management should have a different list of priorities during a transformation process than during normal, everyday business.

Success also rests on a number of other factors. We believe the following are particularly important:

- *Live out tomorrow's world today*
  The future must be tangible. Employees need to see quick wins, but they must also experience the new organization right from day one. A classic mistake here is to announce changes but then fall back into the old patterns of behavior during the process of implementation. If management doesn't start acting differently straight away, staff are unlikely to believe that things will change later on. Top management must live out what they expect from their staff. If they expect others to be prepared to change, but stick to their old ways themselves, they damage the credibility of the whole concept. Thus, for example, if a company aspires to a culture of integration, it can't leave the planning and implementation of the change management exclusively to the management: it must enable staff to be involved on a broad basis.

- *Make staff experience the change*
  If the workforce see from their own experience that the changes affect everyone equally, then they will be more willing to participate in the change process. Thus it is a good idea to start the restructuring and reorganization in as many different areas as possible at the same time. This will stop staff feeling that some people are allowed to their old behavior patterns, while they themselves have to go to the bother of changing.
  Changing as many things as possible at the same time also creates the feeling that the company is undergoing a total remake. It forces the company to reorient itself in a positive way and so improves flexibility – provided, of course, that the change process is properly coordinated and directed toward consistent targets.

- *Have an overall game plan*
  It is essential that top management works out clearly what the best model for the organization is as a whole, i.e. the overarching elements that bind the individual, decentralized units together. This is a key part of a successful restructuring strategy. Here, the trust-based organization comes into its own. It integrates decentralized market strength high up in the company through a combination of management principles, benchmarking guidelines, culture

and such like, and thus allows it to contribute its full potential. Where individual change programs are necessary, due to specific differences between units, top management must ensure that they form part of a general overall game plan and thus contribute to the development of the organization as a whole.

- *Ensure the right attitude*
  As we have seen, a successful change process relies on the active participation of top management and appropriate communication following on from this. However, total transformation is too big a project to be carried out only by the people at the top. People are needed at every level who are open to change and can drive the change process forward. Throughout the organization people must understand that change is expected and know what they have to do about it. Only then can the mobilization of the organization begin.

- *Avoid a flash in the pan*
  Change management is only effective if it has clear targets that are backed up with quantitative measures. General descriptions of management's expectations or vaguely-worded objectives do not generate commitment: they lead to avoidance strategies. Only that which can be (and is) measured, gets changed.

- *Don't change strategy*
  For change management to be successful, you follow the same strategy consistently throughout the whole process. Constant tinkering will make the workforce insecure and ultimately lead to change fatigue. Management must therefore make careful preparation for the change management process and then constantly check that the planned (and communicated) course is being followed.

- *Change skills – use them or lose them*
  You can't learn change skills in the abstract: you need to learn them hands-on. You also need to keep working on them, otherwise you risk losing them. Organizations must cultivate the relevant know-how internally. Flexibility is increasingly called for today, and change skills are therefore a valuable resource in avoiding (potentially costly) mistakes. Individuals with these skills in the organization should act as multipliers, not just passing on their knowledge in seminars, but also giving practical guidance to the people currently managing change processes. Broad-based integration – i.e. a serious attitude to participation – will widen the circle of people in the know.

Incidentally, it is worth noting that trust-based organizations admit when they make mistakes. It is often said that a change process has to be 100% perfect to be accepted by the workforce. Not so. Change must be dynamic, and changes in planning are just as possible as changes in the external environment. Change management must have a mechanism for correcting mistakes and adapting to new situations – management should openly communicate this and take a relaxed approach to conflicts (without trivializing the importance of conflict resolution, of course). If they do, staff will see that the change process is not about implementing a preset plan come what may, but about having the chance to experience entrepreneurship in its very best form.

This is not to say that companies can take a happy-go-lucky attitude toward mistakes. Slipshod work of the part of management will be instantly recognized by those affected. A company that announces a change program without having identified the milestones that will need to be met, quickly loses the trust of its employees and hence the lever for mobilizing them. Books on management theory state that in many companies the change process lacks an ultimate objective. This is borne out by our own experience working with clients. In other words, companies often fail to identify and evaluate the potential growth fields and efficiency levers. As a result, they have no long-term plausible basis for building a "story". And a good story forms the basis for any change process: it is what is needed to bring the otherwise dry, numbers-based management process to life.

The 4Cs – The Toolbox for Change Management

At Roland Berger Strategy Consultants, we have broad experience supporting companies through change processes. This expertise has been distilled into a model that brings together the four key elements involved in mobilizing the workforce, which we call the "4Cs for change" (see Figure 31). As we have seen, mobilizing people is the true objective of any change management directed toward the dual goal of growth and operational excellence; only a mobilized workforce will be open to changes, as well as flexible and committed. If a strategy is going to work in a competitive market – i.e. bring economic success – it needs to be brought to life by the workforce. This means making changes in four distinct areas:

Content	Commitment	Capabilities	Culture
• Corporate audit (strategy, operations) • Target systems/metrics • Mission statement • Cultural audit (staff survey) • Large group intervention/ open space sessions • Management conferences • Internal communication (cascades, target-group-specific channels) • External communication	• Management by objectives • Appraisal systems (e.g. 360-degree feedback) • Remuneration and incentives • Reward management • Management audit • Feedback using opinion barometers, discussion events, etc.	• Efficient program/project management • Coaching • Teambuilding/team effectiveness • Competence models • Training sessions/human resources development • Leadership development • Education monitoring • Tests/analyses of potential	• Leadership guidelines • Quality management • Learning organization/ know-how management • Job structuring (job rotation, job enrichment) • Team structures (e.g., semi-autonomous work groups) • Change monitoring

Fig. 31: Measures for mobilizing the workforce as part of a change management process

Content – Communicate the Change

Good communication is open, honest and timely. This is a cornerstone of the trust-based organization – and with good reason. Even during a phase of reconstruction, it is essential that companies communicate as much as possible. And high quality communication doesn't just give the necessary facts and information: it also speaks to the hearts of the employees. In a Europe-wide study carried out in conjunction with the INSEAD Business School, we discovered that the key is not only communicating the objectives of the transformation, but also a vision. This vision serves as a long-term point of orientation. For this process to be successful – i.e. for the workforce to be convinced and motivated – the vision must "come to life" during the course of the change management process. If, on the other hand, top management and the marketing department just come up with some fancy-sounding slogans, the workforce will be unconvinced and the success of the change management process put at risk.

Management must communicate substance, not slogans, both before and during the change management process. As well as talking about the vision and explaining how target fulfillment will be measured, they should also ask the employees directly about their hopes and expectations, and then respond accordingly.

Our joint study with INSEAD revealed that companies are critical of their own communication processes. They know where the improvement potential lies and which parts of the processes need special attention. In particular, they stressed the importance of using communication throughout the change process to maintain a sense of urgency, giving fuller, clearer information about the desired result of the process and communicating on a more personal level earlier on.

Commitment – Add Incentives

Change can only work if the members of the organization are convinced that it is urgently needed. A wave of motivation must pass through the whole company, driving the change process forward on all levels. This is generated by top management setting an example that is then passed down through the entire hierarchy. Middle management, in particular, play a crucial role as multipliers. However, our joint study with INSEAD identifies a problem here: middle management is often critical of the change processes. One of the reasons is that middle managers often think in the context of their own departments and so fail to see the big picture. If companies want to ensure their support, they should therefore create incentives such as bonuses or the prospect of promotion, as well as arguing the case for the change process. These incentives should be based on a system of target agreements with strict targets that fulfill a number of criteria. In particular, they must be:

- *Specific:* Targets can be influenced by the individual and must show specifically how actions relate to results.

- *Measurable:* The expected results are described exactly so that there is no doubt whether targets have been met or not.

- *Action-oriented:* Targets are linked to specific actions supporting the change process.

- *Relevant:* Targets are relevant to the change process and thus provide it with the right orientation.

- *Time-framed:* The time frame for meeting targets is clear.

Capabilities – Develop Skills

The emphasis here is on developing two different types of skills. The first type are skills that stimulate and have a positive impact on the change process: first and foremost, the social and communication skills of managers and staff. Companies must train up the "change leaders" – the individuals who will drive the change management process ahead by heading task forces, running workshops, acting as multipliers and so on. Change leaders also need motivation in the form of incentives and career prospects that extend beyond the change period itself. New forms of cooperation should also be encouraged, such as building networks within the organization or with external partners.

The second type of skills are those that will be required once the transformation process is complete. The company should determine exactly what these skills are, and to what extent each of them will be needed. It can then start building them up in a targeted way. Otherwise, the company may hit a skills bottleneck later on that cannot be solved by hiring new staff.

Culture – Build a Culture

Finally, it is necessary to create an organizational framework that promotes the company's ability and willingness to change over the long term. A trust-based organization is the ideal model here as it combines the necessary flexibility with a practical incentive – the challenge of working together to further develop the company.

The right culture must be firmly rooted in the organization. This means more than just lip service: the desired culture must be translated into concrete targets that are then monitored to check whether they are being met or not. Accordingly, at the beginning of the change management process, the company should examine the existing corporate culture. This can be done, for example, by means of an employee survey which provides a picture of the current mood in the company and reveals the underlying values. Relevant cultural dimensions for examination include cooperation, the attitude to work, processes, leadership, communication and information.

Identifying the corporate culture is usually done by means of a written survey distributed to a representative section of employees and backed up with more in-depth interviews. The survey is then repeated during, or at the end of, the change process and thus functions as a monitoring tool.

Planning a Comprehensive Transformation Process

The "4Cs for change" indicate the different areas involved in a change process and show what exactly the program should consist of. As we have seen, the change process must embrace the entire organization – just working on a few weak points within the company will not generate the necessary momentum and mobilize the workforce to action. Top management must aim at a comprehensive transformation of the entire organization, as this is its only hope of truly anchoring the dual strategy of ability and willingness to grow within the company. The ultimate objective of everything that happens during the course of the transformation process is to root the necessary flexibility deep in the organization's value system and processes. This flexibility then allows the company to resolve the apparent strategic contradiction between, on the one hand cost, optimization and operational excellence, and, on the other, a future-oriented growth program (see Figure 32).

To ensure a comprehensive transformation – that is to say, one that operates on a number of fronts with different teams working in parallel – companies need to follow a three-stage plan. This plan follows Lewin's change theory. First, it opens up the workforce to the idea of change (i.e. prepares them for the transformation). Then it guides them through the change process. And finally it consolidates the changes that have been made. Companies can use this plan to generate the necessary mobilization, as it gives employees the feeling that they are being taken seriously and fully involved in the change process.

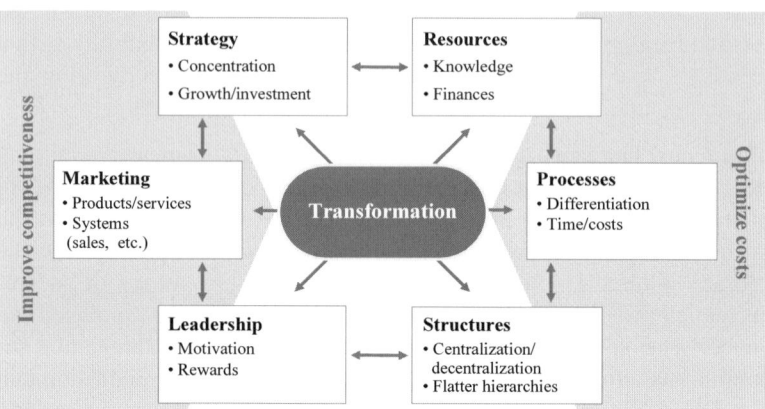

Fig. 32: Transformation – an integrated concept for implementing the dual strategy of growth and restructuring

Figure 33 is a model of the three-stage plan. The first phase is that of initiating the transformation. This involves determining what changes are required with regards to corporate strategy by means of analyses (processes, functions, management, organization etc.) and benchmarking (competition, neighboring industries), and then deciding on the line of attack. To do this, it is essential that the company knows what the key issues are regarding growth plans, innovation projects, efficiency improvements and so on. Phase one also involves setting up the necessary measuring and steering systems, as well as the operational and organizational structure, in preparation for the actual transformation phase. At the end of the initial phase, the company should draw up a detailed change concept. This gives the exact targets and provides the workforce with a "story" for the transformation.

The second phase sets the change process in motion. Practical measures and projects begin in as many different parts of the organization as possible. To ensure the necessary level of acceptance, the company should place great emphasis on changing the corporate culture: simply relying on the chosen instruments to do their job is not enough. The cultural change must take place during this phase – if it fails, the whole transformation process is at risk of failing.

Quick wins can have a lasting effect here by demonstrating to employees that the effort involved in implementing the transformation is worthwhile for all. In addition, management should not only announce a new culture of open communication but also establish it through their own example, making it binding for everyone. Communication measures are particular important in this phase since the deep-going changes will inevitably give rise to criticism in some quarters. This can have a negative effect on the general level of acceptance of the changes and create difficulties for the project as a whole.

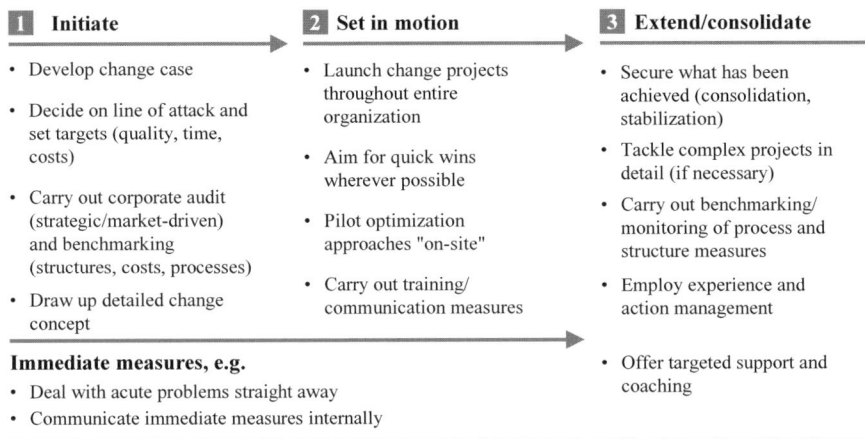

Fig. 33: Three phases of the transformation process

The final phase is concerned with consolidating the transformation. If necessary, the change process can still be extended with selected measures, or the company can wait until this phase to tackle more complex projects in detail. The company must now have achieved the necessary combination of ability and willingness to grow and should be certain that the workforce is ready to "shift up a gear" and initiate dynamic processes.

Of course, when it comes to transformation there is no one-size-fits-all. Every change project is unique and must be individually crafted. However, breaking the process up into three phases is a tried and tested method that involves ever greater numbers of employees in each stage of the process. It also, crucially, enables the company to find the right balance between growth-driven and restructuring projects.

Successful transformation is the only way to turn a company into a decentralized, trust-based organization and hence put it on a course to combined growth and restructuring. We have seen what is needed to make it successful: the transformation must be comprehensive, involve both operations and strategy, contain elements of restructuring and elements that point forward, be credible, and above all be able to mobilize the workforce. Quite a tall order. But if a company manages the difficult job of transforming itself successfully, it will be amply rewarded in terms of improved stability, productivity and competitiveness.

The Macroeconomic Perspective

So far, we have only looked at microeconomic phenomena and the growth strategies pursued by companies. Obviously these are of interest for managers and consultants, for professional reasons. But it is also worth looking at the wider economic context: after all, corporate growth also has an impact on a country's economy. If companies are not growing, the economy cannot prosper. However, the same is true the other way round: The overall conditions that companies find in the countries where they operate are of great significance.

Creating the right conditions to stimulate business growth both short and long term is a challenge faced by politics, society and the economy. There are three key things they must do. The first is to increase competitiveness, for example by letting companies agree wages individually rather than fixing them on a national basis, and by encouraging business start-ups and eliminating red-tape. The second is to raise flexibility, for example by adjusting regulations on laying off workers, adding more variable elements to salaries and creating more flexible contracts. And the third is to promote innovation, for example by investing more in education, supporting life-long learning and promoting partnerships between academia and business.

We have seen how companies discuss growth – but how do countries do it? Like companies, they use a series of indicators that look at economic development within the borders of their country. They also face similar pressure to grow. Where business has the Fortune 500 list, countries have economic indicators, international statistics on unemployment, comparisons of national debt and export performance figures. Bodies such as the World Economic Forum (WEF) in Geneva and the Institute for Management Development (IMD) in neighboring Lausanne publish annual surveys of countries' competitiveness, based on several hundred indicators. But above all, a macroeconomic perspective looks at two things. The first is the total performance of all the companies in a particular country. And the second is the performance of the State and public authorities, regulatory and economic policy, and the quantity and quality of the infrastructure – in short, the ability of a country to provide companies with the necessary framework for economic development.

Today's managers cannot run their companies using the recipes and tools of the 1970s or '80s. The same goes for economic policy. It too, operates in an international environment that has changed massively and which continues to show dynamic change. New actors are constantly rewriting the rules. Over the last ten to fifteen years, individual countries have reacted very differently to the new circumstances. There is still room for maneuver – countries have their own options and choices to make. And the resulting picture is a mixed one: some countries have adapted excellently, while others have not been able to keep up across the board.

This is clear from a comparison of various international indicators; it can also be seen in terms of growth and prosperity.

For European companies it is the European economic area as a whole rather than the national business environment that is becoming ever more important with regard to business conditions. Despite globalization, the European home market continues to be of overwhelming importance for companies. In fact, the largest European companies generate on average 63% of their sales within the European market. Only 3% of the world's biggest 500 companies are truly global, with an equal spread of sales across the triad regions Asia, North America and Europe. Hence, a favorable home market remains a key success factor for the growth of companies. The common European market with its 455m consumers, its large buying power, and its common cultural roots and institutional framework thus provides good ground for companies to grow.

Despite these favorable conditions, the EU 15 countries have shown sluggish economic growth of about 1.4% p.a. during the past five years. Especially large European countries are lagging behind. The German economy grew by only 0.7% p.a. between 2000 and 2005, and was even undercut by Italy with 0.6% per annum. By contrast, smaller countries like Finland, Sweden, and Ireland managed to grow much faster, with average annual growth rates between 2.2% p.a. (Sweden) and 5.3% p.a. (Ireland). However, by and large, Europe as a whole grew much slower than the U.S. and still continues to miss the initial Lisbon target of 3% economic growth per annum.

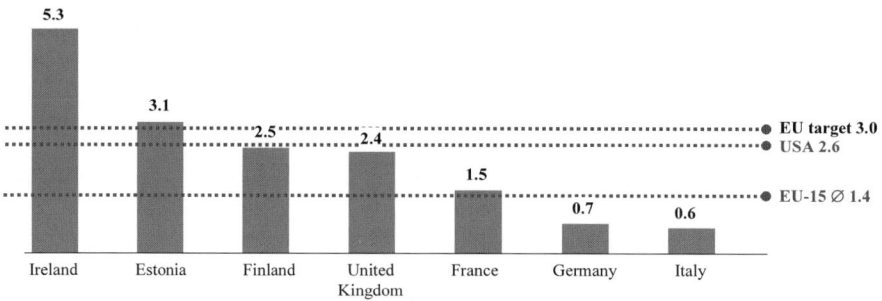

Fig. 34: Average growth of real GDP 2000-2005 [% p.a.] (Source: Economist Intelligence Unit)

So the obvious question is, can companies grow *in spite of* the conditions in their home country? Evidently they can. In some important industries, European companies clearly outperformed their international competitors. For example, European automotive companies managed to increase their sales by 8.0% p.a. since 2000, while their American counterparts only raised their sales by 0.7% p.a. on average. Also chemicals and telecom grew faster in Europe than in the U.S. or in Japan. Moreover, in many industries, European companies are more profitable than their U.S. counterparts: For example, average returns at chemical companies in Europe are 5.2%, compared with only 3.4% in the United States. European companies also do better in the energy sector and in automotive (see figure 35). These results stem from a number of strengths that European companies can rely on.

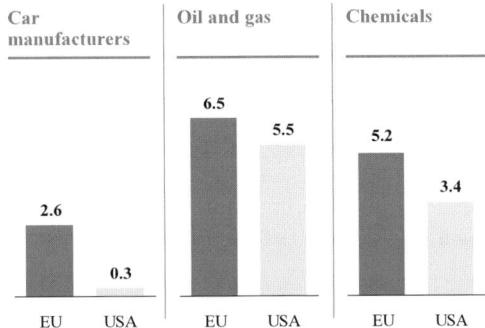

Fig. 35: Return on sales after tax in different industries 2005 [% p.a.] (Source: Fortune Global 500, Bloomberg)

First, European companies are leading when it comes to innovation. Taking research-intensive industries as a whole, Europe has an R&D-intensive share of 8.3% of added value – and is thus clearly ahead of the U.S.'s 7.9%. Furthermore, Europe also employs more people in these future-oriented sectors: 6.9% in the EU-15 versus only 4.9% in the United States.

Second, European companies have used their strong position on their home markets to go further and tap the potential of worldwide markets. Europe's exports represent 38.5% of all global exports, since European economies are much more export-oriented than the United States, with an export ratio of 37.3% of GDP on average in 2005, opposed to 10.4% in the U.S. Of course, these results of European companies do not only derive from export efforts, but from setting up production facilities and branches abroad. At Siemens, for example, 247,000 out of 417,000 employees work in other countries than Germany, and the same is true for Vivendi where the share of foreign employment sums up to 65% of total employment.

Third, European companies have clear competitive advantages in several areas. According to an annual study carried out by the World Economic Forum, companies from some European countries are in a commanding position when it comes to sophistication of product processes, uniqueness of products and processes, control of international distribution, and the extent of staff training.

In other words: European companies are doing well, but nevertheless, as a location for business, Europe can't quite get off the ground. So the question is, how long can firms continue to grow in spite of their home region? And – taking into account the rising share of employment abroad – at what cost to the corresponding countries? With seasonally adjusted unemployment hovering around the 17 million mark in the EU 25 in Summer 2006 and a chronically unbalanced budget in some countries, it seems clear that what the European economy needs is the same as its companies: a combination of the ability and willingness to grow. This is the only way to ensure that everyone can participate in society and, on this basis, enjoy minimum social protection. Below, we take a closer look at Europe's chances and prospects as a location for business in terms of these two key concepts – the ability and willingness to grow.

Macroeconomic Ability to Grow

It is generally held that Europe offers good structural conditions for business in a variety of fields: its physical infrastructure, quality of research, environment, provision of capital to businesses, highly qualified workforce, and so forth. However, there is no reason for Europe to rest on its own laurels. A number of policies have to be improved if Europe wants to keep up with its competitors.

What is perhaps most important in this regard is the improvement of educational systems within the European Union. As mentioned above, Europe's competitive advantages do not derive from cheap labor but from the ability to differentiate oneself in the marketplace through unique products and processes and innovative solutions. The pre-requisite for these advantages is a highly qualified workforce that is able to fully understand production technologies and service processes that are becoming ever more complex. Unfortunately, spending on education varies significantly among EU member states, and so does participation in life-long learning. Countries like Finland or Sweden invest about 7% of their gross domestic product in the education of human resources, while in Greece education expenditures amount to less than 4% of GDP. Taking into account that the risk of unemployment decreases with the number of years of education, there is no doubt that European countries must improve their educational systems if they want to exploit their labor force potential and achieve high economic growth rates. This is especially true because also emerging countries are more and more recognizing the value of education for economic success. Hence, we do not only need more money, but – what is even more important – also a culture that recognizes and values the importance of education and life-long learning.

In order to achieve sustainable growth rates, Europe also has to improve its performance in terms of innovation. The Lisbon goals strived at spending 3% of GDP on research and development on average. Although it does by no means come as a surprise that innovation policy is critical to ensure competitiveness vis-à-vis emerging economies, most European countries continue to miss this important target. Hence, innovation policy has to be improved on the national as well as on the European level.

Striving for sustainable growth by successful research and development policies of course means diverting current spending. Rather than financing the past or trying to preserve the present (e.g. by spending on the welfare state), Europe must invest in the future. Currently, government interference is still high in Europe. This not only diverts spending from important policy fields, but is also distorting competition and preventing the discovery of new, more intelligent solutions. Today, subsidies in European countries still sum up to 1.2% of GDP on average, ranging from 0.6% in Great Britain and Ireland to 2.9% in Austria. Many of these subsidies flow into industries that lack future growth potential (which is basically why they need subsidies). In most of these cases, government intervention is achieving nothing but slowing down structural change and thus undermining long-term competitiveness. The same goes for the European level: Still, the lion's share of the EU's financial support benefits the primary sector – which is, to say the least, very inappropriate.

In line with this argumentation, European competitive policy has to become gutsier. Short-term oriented protectionism as seen with regard to the European services directive that was subject to not less than 213 modifications in Spring 2006 within the European Parliament does by no means contribute to future competitiveness and wealth. Also with regard to infrastructure industries, a withdrawal of the state – going hand in hand with a thorough re-regulation in order to avoid the replacement of state monopolies by private monopolies – is overdue. Of course, under certain circumstances, government regulation can contribute to innovation – consider for example product market regulation or environmental standards that trigger more efficient production technologies. But by and large, economic theory has shown that market solutions prove to be more sustainable and efficient than government solutions.

The latter is especially true with regard to bureaucracy, the natural enemy of entrepreneurial spirit. Officialdom interferes excessively with economic activity. According to calculations carried out by the World Bank starting a business is much easier within the OECD countries on average than it is in Europe. It takes five days in the U.S. to start your business while it takes twice as long in Europe on average – a level of government interference that significantly hampers the ability of European companies, and hence the European economy, to grow.

To come to the point: Europe has to replace its traditional economic policy by a modern economic policy. This means especially enhancing the development of regional economic clusters that ensure knowledge spill-overs between business and science. This can be done not only by investing in research and education but also by taking care that different actors from the field of science as well as the field of business get together. Doing so will by far more contribute to economic growth than, for example, protecting so-called 'national champions'. The emergence of these economic clusters, especially in future growth industries like biotechnology or aerospace, can trigger future growth of companies as well as of the economy as a whole.

Clearly, Europe has some problems with its ability to grow. In our view, Europe's ability to grow will not improve as a result of short-term measures. What is needed is a comprehensive program with appropriate long-term goals. This aspect is lacking in the current social and political debate, which aims at quick successes in areas such as reducing unemployment. Fundamental improvements in the relevant indicators can only come on the back of a broad-based reform program.

Macroeconomic Willingness to Grow

In order to agree on these broad-based reform programs, countries need to be not just able, but also willing to grow. Society's willingness to grow can be seen in its openness toward growth processes – its readiness to make the extra effort that means the difference between average and excellent growth performance.

A country's economy cannot grow unless society shows a readiness to take risks, courage to change, self-belief, optimism and trust. The link between economic growth and trust is supported by empirical evidence: recent economic studies have shown that interpersonal trust has a substantial impact on economic growth. Greater trust from a social point of view also means lower transaction costs and hence a greater willingness to invest. The reverse is also true: a lack of trust leads to more risk and insecurity, and hence less willingness to invest. Ultimately, the country can fall into a growth trap caused by mistrust. Trust is also a powerful stimulant in countries with developing economies. Thus an increase of 15% in the number of people who consider their country trustworthy generates permanent growth of 1% in per capita GDP. And this growth is self-perpetuating: the higher income levels in turn lead to more trust, and so it goes on.

To a certain extent, Europe lacks the necessary mindset of trust and optimism. And the problem starts right at the top. Here's an example. German top managers begin a SWOT analysis by looking at their weaknesses and threats, and only then (if they're still feeling strong) do they examine their strengths. American managers do the opposite. First, they look at their strengths and opportunities and then they turn to their threats. This just about sums up the problem with willingness to grow in at least some European countries.

Of course, values differ a lot between different European countries. However, a certain lack of confidence concerning the future cannot be denied. A survey carried out by Eurostat in 2006 showed that 39 percent of Europeans believe that their economy will impair within the next twelve months. In Germany, even 49 percent of respondents think so. It does not come as a surprise that this lack of optimism has a knock-on effect on buying behavior of consumers and investment of companies: Economic theory shows a clear correlation between expectations and economic development.

Closely related with rather negative expectations, mistrust in political and economic elites is widely spread. Another survey carried out by the Gesellschaft für Konsumforschung in 2005 showed that only 32 percent of Europeans have faith in managers. Only politicians are trusted less (14 percent), while e.g. 85 percent have trust in physicians. What is perhaps noteworthy is that, again, the Scandinavian countries perform best with regard to trust: After all, 51 percent of all Swedes have faith in their managerial elite.

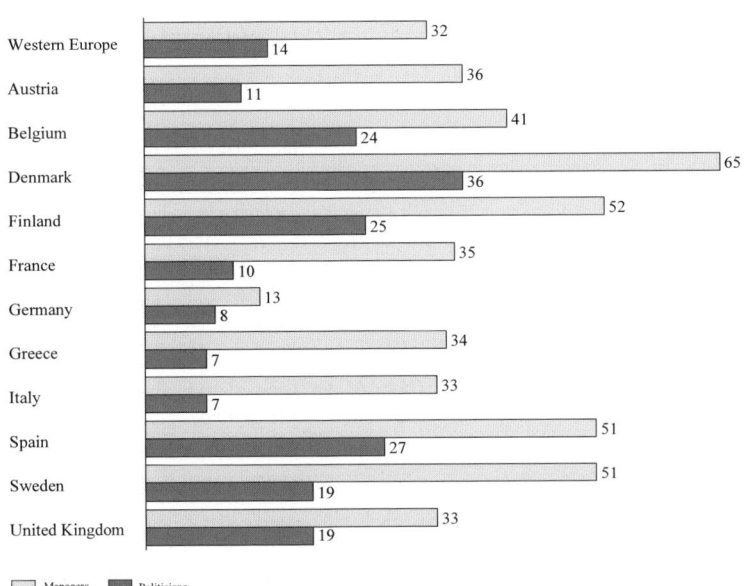

Fig. 36: Survey results on trust in Europe 2005 [% of respondents] (Source: GfK)

So when it comes to the willingness to grow, at least some European countries have deficits in many areas. Horst Siebert, longstanding member of the German Council of Economic Experts, summarizes them as follows: "You can't have growth without entrepreneurs – and certainly not *in spite of* them. Whether we get enough dynamic entrepreneurs depends crucially on the social environment and many soft factors, how willing society is to take risks, the attitude toward technology, the openness toward new things, the social acceptability of profit, the value placed on entrepreneurial activity by society, the readiness to compete and the trust placed in the markets."

Europe has clearly proved its willingness to take risks in the past. Agreeing on the Single market was anything but risk averse, and so was the introduction of the European Monetary Union that did take place without past comparison. Not to mention the Eastward enlargement that brought forward an integration of ten countries that were totally different in economic terms. In short: The history of European economic integration is a history of braveness. If the same is true for the future, Europe will surely manage to combine the ability and the willingness to grow.

Epilogue

Growth is not an end in itself. So the question is, who does a company grow for? On the one hand, it grows in order to serve customers, to beat the competition, to give investors a return on their investment and to create jobs. But it also grows simply in order to survive as a company. It is the process-related and intellectual skills within a company that make it strong – its team spirit, its innovative strength, its networks and often also its brand. If it fails to grow, all of these are at risk, because stagnation leads to a direct reduction in the scope for investment in these areas. Companies that do not grow lose their best people. And successful teams cannot be simply bought in: they need to be built up and tended with care and patience. If any piece in the puzzle is missing, the balance is upset. So without growth, the basis for future growth is eroded.

In essence, growth is always about development. Although you can measure it in terms of quantity, growth is actually just as much about quality. So pushing up sales is not enough in itself: the precondition for lasting success is transforming the organization. What happens when companies simply grow in quantitative terms can be seen from the experience with the e-economy. When the Internet bubble burst, it immediately became obvious that two important aspects had been missing: profit (and in many cases even sales) and organizational scalability. Companies lacked staff who could implement their rather vague ideas. Their rudimentary organizational structures did not provide a stable basis for growth. It was a classic case of "diseconomies of speed": without the necessary qualities to cope with rapid expansion, growth soon comes to a standstill.

This demonstrates that growth is, in fact, a separate business process. It must be strategically planned in advance and then carefully managed during its implementation. The reason is that the growth process is the determining factor behind all other corporate processes. Firms that have understood this make growth an independent core strategic competency. They view their practical experience (gained during the course of regional expansion, acquisitions and integration, product launches, etc.) as strategic growth expertise and focus on expanding this in a targeted way. In addition, they create special areas of responsibility for growth projects within the top management, whose job it is to implement the relevant (economic, organizational, legal) knowledge within the organization.

Managed in this way, the growth algorithm can begin to operate. This is a self-perpetuating process that gains in strength as it proceeds. Companies that make growth a core strategic competency have recognized that progress is only possible if accompanied by continuous restructuring. Restructuring activities are a prerequisite for being fit for expansion and go hand-in-hand with the ongoing development of the organization – which means striving toward efficient management processes that can master the growing complexity. This is all the more important since many outperformers prefer a special organizational model: the decentralized organization. In this model, market-related processes enjoy a high level of independence and responsibility. At the same time, any processes that offer economies of scale are kept central (or bought in from third parties) so as to exploit volume synergies. A decentralized organization thus makes efficient use of lower transaction costs while avoiding diseconomies of scale.

Trust is the only possible integrator in such a corporate structure. For trust to appear, companies must combine their economic interests with a moral element. And this must happen on every level of the business: within the organization itself, in the form of transparency toward partners in the value chain, investors and customers and in the company's willingness to learn and develop. Trust is commitment that the company must make itself. This is where the greatest challenge lies. The recent past has shown us that businesses cannot survive without a moral element: companies must implement a new ethical, communication and operating concept if they want to grow.

On a microeconomic scale, there is no upper limit on growth in principle. Managers often blame a period of stagnation on the "difficult economic situation". This is what is commonly known as spin. The real problem is a lack of strategic and operational excellence on the part of management. Take a closer look and you can find examples of companies showing outstanding growth in all industries and markets whatever the economic trend.

However, companies do face internal barriers to growth. Chief among them is a lack of willingness to grow: the structures and processes for growth are in place but the desire is lacking. Motivation is what makes the difference. Without it, organizations are not willing to make the effort to grow. To a large extent, therefore, successful growth depends on what is commonly thought of as a "soft", cultural factor. Here, once again, we see the increasing influence of non-economic factors on business indicators and decisions. This factor must be integrated into the business model. And the best way to do this is with a trust-based organization, as this connects all the necessary levels in an integrated way. Rather than sporadic actions in response to individual challenges, the trust-based organization has individual building blocks that it arranges into an integrated whole. This has two advantages. Firstly, the physical and cultural investments made by the organization bring long-term returns, rather than a one-off effect. And secondly, the organization gains a certain immunity to challenges of all different sorts thanks to its overall concept and the logical basis underlying it. Both these factors place the company in an excellent position within the current global economic context.

Of all the challenges facing companies, growth offers the richest rewards. Making growth work is the only way for companies today to build their reputation and ensure their profits. The curtain has gone up – it's time for the show to begin!